BEGINNING & END

Poetry in lamentation and celebration of the Holy Household

Nouri Sardar

Copyright © 2014 by The Universal Muslim Association of America
1717 Pennsylvania Ave NW #1025
Washington, DC 20006.
Phone: 202-559-9123
Email: info@umaamerica.net
Brought to you by The UMAA Publishing House.
All rights reserved. No part of this publication may be reproduced, distributed, or transmitted in any form or by any means, including photocopying, recording, or other electronic or mechanical methods, without the prior written permission of the publisher, except in the case of brief quotations embodied in critical reviews and certain other noncommercial uses permitted by copyright law.

Printed in the United States of America

ISBN-13: 978-1500600105
ISBN-10: 1500600105

DEDICATION

In the name of God, most Gracious, most Merciful

"Verily, there are various degrees of serving Allah, but affection for us, AhlulBayt, is the highest one."

- Imam Jafar Al-Sadiq

NOURI SARDAR

Contents

Introduction 1
THE HOUSEHOLD CARVED IN GOLD 9
Poetry in memory of the holiest household 9
Beginning & End 11
Everything Within Me 13
My Greatest Deed 15
Iraq's Shrines 17
Opening Verses II 19
THE MASTER OF CREATION 23
Poetry in memory of the holy Prophet Mohammed (pbuh) 23
The Garden 25
This is Mohammed 27
Unspoken 29
In Their Eyes 31
One of a Kind 33
All That Rises 35
THE PEAK OF ELOQUENCE 37
Poetry in memory of the Commander of the Faithful (pbuh) 37
A Glimpse of Ali 39
The Difference 43
Your Sweet Name 45
My First is Ali 47
Do Not Hate Me 49
Ali in 60 Seconds 51
Martyred in Prayer 53

All My Patience 57
The Sound of Thunder 59
When the Body Dies 63
With His Final Breath 67
Sons of Ali & Hussain 71
Najaf 73
I Ask You By Ali 75
By the Son of Ali 77
Ali's My First Imam 79

THE LADY OF LIGHT 81
Poetry in memory of the leader of women of all worlds (pbuh) 81
I Am Muslim 83
In Her Grave 85
Remembered 87
The Tragedy of Fatima Zahra 89
Tonight 91
Another Day 93
Piece of Heaven 95
How Many Women Fall? 97
Forgive Me 99
If You Had Known 101
Marriage of Ali and Fatima 103

THE UNDYING FLAME 105
Poetry in memory of the Master of Martyrs (pbuh) 105
Opening Verses III (Muharram) 107
Your Day 109
Hussain's Worth 113
Silent I Leave 115

- Jibraeel's Wings 117
- A Heartbreaking Goodbye 121
- The Killing - Al Maqtal 123
- Crying in My Sleep 125
- A Promise 129
- Hussain Never Died 131
- Every Moment 135
- With Your Love 137
- This Wound 139
- My Life is Two Names 141
- A Thousand Years 143
- I'm from Heaven 147
- Our Beloved's Praise 149
- Revolution in the Heart 153
- Changing of the Flag 155
- Take Me 157
- If You Visit 159
- Forty Days 163
- The Road to Karbala 167
- Nothing Will Stop Me 169
- Karbala's Month 171

THE GUARDIAN OF THE VEIL 173
Poetry in memory of the Father of Virtues (pbuh) 173
- In Awe of You 175
- The Moon Descends 179
- Water I Threw Away 183
- Abbas-Ali 187
- This is the Farewell 189

    Just Forget Me 191

    If Abbas Sends Back Your Wish 193

    Under the Care of Abbas 195

THE MOTHER OF CALAMITY 197

  Poetry in memory of Zainab (pbuh) 197

    End of Times 199

    By the Blood of Hussain 201

    I See 203

    In A Poem 205

    I Remembered Zahra 207

THE IMMORTAL DAY 211

  Poetry in memory of the family and companions of 211

  Imam Hussain that were martyred or left in loss on the day of Ashura (Peace be upon them all) 211

    Will I Recall You? 213

    Kufa to Karbala 215

    The Angel of Death in Kufa 217

    The Ansar 219

    The Awaited Visit 221

    Qassim's Request 225

    I Prepared Him Honey 229

    Goodbye Qassim 231

    Stay 233

    I Lament 235

    For What Sin? 239

    To Najaf I Turn 241

THE SYMBOL OF PATIENCE 243

  Poetry in memory Lady Ummul Baneen 243

(Peace be upon her)) 243
 Gave Away My Hands 245
 All of My Sons 247
 Alone 249
 Called Me Ummul Baneen 251
 Remember Her 253

THE IMMORTAL GUIDANCE 257
Poetry in memory of the Imams of the Holy Household 257
(Peace be upon them) 257
 Let Me Show You Jaber 259
 My Treaty of Rights 261
 Where Are the Shia? 263
 King of Hearts 265
 Jawad's Ship 267
 What Happened? 269

THE AWAITED 273
Poetry in memory of the Twelfth Imam 273
(May the Almighty hasten his reappearance) 273
 Before I Leave 275
 Which Door? 277
 In Mehdi's Eyes 279
 Ali's Door 283
 Imam Mehdi 285
 Ziyarat Karbala 289

About the Writer 293
About the Publisher 297

Introduction

In the name of Allah, Most Gracious, Most Merciful

For every beginning, there is an end. Both define us, and reflect the short life we live in between. Our beginning is made for us; we have no choice with regard to it, whilst the value of our end is defined by the actions of our own hands.

This book, my fourth volume of collected poetry, suggests that our beginning is the Prophet Muhammad (peace and blessings be upon him and his family), as he opened our minds with his teachings and words, gave us the perfect code for existence - that being the religion of our divine Lord - and informed us of the purpose behind that same existence, to worship this same Lord.

It also suggests that our end is the awaited saviour of our time, the grandson of this holy Prophet (pbuh) - Imam Mehdi (may the Lord hasten his reappearance), as he will remind us of this same message, reopen the minds that have been closed by centuries of disobedience to the Creator and disregard for humanity, and reignite the flame of belief in the purpose of our existence, that has become almost dormant since the time of his grandfather.

Essentially, it suggests that our beginning, end, and everything in between, is the holy Prophet Muhammad and his glorious household (may peace and blessings be upon them all).

This volume is another humble contribution in honour of the personalities, characters and lives of these historic figures, who gave all for the sake of the betterment of humanity.

Once again, it contains poems that aim to make you cry, make you smile, but overall re-instil that love and obedience to this Household from which the perfect human being and perfect worshipper of his Lord can be derived. Much like the previous volume, I have tried my best to ensure that the collection in its entirety contributes to reverence of as many personalities from the holy Household as possible.

I discussed the purpose behind my poetry in more detail in the previous volume, so in this introduction I would like to discuss, firstly, the changes that you may find in this volume, and secondly, the mechanics behind the poetry that I write.

With regard to the changes that you will find in this volume, as usual, you will find that the poetry has evolved since the last volume. This book collects my poetry written between late 2012 and early 2013. As discussed previously, it is natural that the poetry has become stronger, more in-depth and more creative, simply due to the fact that talent evolves with time.

What I considered as a good poem years ago, is not what I consider as a good poem today, and will not be what I consider as a good poem years from now, that is, if Allah (Subhanuhu wa Ta'ala) allows me to continue writing and grants me success. Another change that you may notice is that the poetry is now divided into two categories: 'In Lamentation' and 'In Celebration'.

The lamentations focus on the tragedies of these great personalities, or else are written in such a way, whilst the celebrations seek to, essentially, rejoice the births and characters of these personalities. The main reason for categorising the poems is simply for reciters who are choosing poems to be recited as a lamentation (noha, latmaaya, marthiya or na'ee) or be recited in a joyous occasion (for example, Islamic songs or anasheed), so it is important to note that I do not want these categories to define the poems, rather they are simply there as a manner of reference.

With regard to tuning these poems, I have opted not to include an index which clarifies which tunes each poem was written to, as I feel it may confuse readers both familiar and unfamiliar with the tunes of the Arabic poems/lamentations to which they are written. Furthermore, not all poems are written to a particular tune.

Also, I do not believe a reciter should blindly follow a tune dictated to them, rather they should create a tune that suits both the poem and their voice/method of recitation.

Lastly, I do not want these poems to be limited to such tunes, as over time tunes and recitation techniques shall evolve as new styles are created. An addition that you may notice in this volume is the inclusion of what's called (in Arabic) 'aboothiyat', which I experimented with in the previous volume. These are essentially poems that focus on wordplay as opposed to rhyming.

Now, I would like to discuss the mechanics behind what I write. The purpose of this is to explain how I write, but more importantly to inspire aspiring poets and writers, who can take from the following points what they will.

It will also include my thoughts and opinions and what contributes to a good poem, and what contributes to a bad one (of course, all service toward Allah and the Ahlulbayt is good, however this is all written in critique within the realm of poetry about the holy Household. Furthermore, since poetry is such a vast topic beyond my chosen style of poetry, you a free to take what you feel suits your writing and leave what you feel doesn't).

The first topic of discussion here is rhyming. We find that rhyming can either benefit a poem or destroy a poem. It is important to note that rhymes are meant to compliment poetry and not define its purpose.

The writer must ensure that he/she has control over the rhyme, and that the rhyme doesn't control him/her. If the writer does not have power over the poem, it will be very apparent to the reader who will in turn lose trust in the writer.

Below is an example of what I consider to be the misuse of rhyme:

> I love you O' Hussain
> Daily it brings me pain
> Your love makes me insane
> For you, my tears, they rain

The reason I would consider the above to be a misuse of rhyme is that it gives the impression that the poet has based the sentences of the poem around the rhyme, hence the poem does not have the effect it could have.

As stated, the rhyme only exists to compliment, therefore it must be the sentence that takes priority over the rhyme. This can be achieved by putting thought into the reason we are including the rhyming word we have chosen, and what we aim to portray.

Below is an example of how I would write the poem, using the same rhymes:

> The heart beats daily: 'Hussain'
> Flowing in blood, soothing pain
> In your love crazed and insane

A servant to a king's reign

The difference in the above is apparent, simply because the reader assumes that a lot of thought has been put into the sentence preceding the rhyme, and what benefit that sentence is going to have to the poem as a whole. Again, if the reader appreciates your control over the words you've written, the poem will have a greater effect on them.

Adding to this, twist of sentence is very popular in poetry. This is because it adds to the idea that poetry does not usually resemble everyday speech. An example would be "the lion of valour you are" - which in common tongue would be spoken as, "you are the lion of valour".

Of course, there is nothing wrong with using it and in fact it is a signature of English poetry, but we must ensure that it is not misused or overused. If it is used, it must be used with purpose, and not for the sake of sounding poetic.

You may find many examples like this throughout this book, due to the fact that I am attempting to instill Eastern rules of rhyme into a very limited language! But regardless, it is important that we keep this in mind.

You will also notice that the poetry I write is written to structures of syllables. This is based on poetry in the East being written to "weight" (wezin). Writing to syllables gives the poem a flow that the reader may subconciously notice. There are a number of typical structures that I write to and all are translations of structures of Arabic poetry, but I will mention two, which I mostly use:

> Brother I woke from a dream... where from me you were absent
> I called your name, no answer... nor did rest with me your scent
> Yet when I woke from this dream... my eyes saw what I had dreamt
> Far from me I saw your flag... and empty I found your tent

The above shows the example of a verse divided into four lines (though this can extend to six or even eight). Each line is split into two separate sentences which would make sense if read alone, and every sentence in the verse is made up of seven syllables (can also be eight). Also, the end of every line rhymes, not the end of every sentence. I find this style of structure very effective as the poet is able to say more in every line.

Below is another type of structure:

> Entranced is every ounce of my own being
> As each step shadows Hussain in me weaving
> My eyes tell me, your heart and mind are dreaming
> I answer, this is your fate you are seeing
> With the tune of his presence so believing
> My soul asks, how can you contemplate leaving?

The above is probably the most typical structure you can find in my poetry and in Eastern poetry. Every line is made up of eleven syllables (but can be twelve) and the number of lines can range from four, to six, to eight. It may be worth noting that the number of lines is always even. Of course, these are examples of the main body of the verses, throughout this book you'll find that choruses also have a big part on the poem, which we shall discuss soon.

Now I would like to discuss content. This is probably the most important section for budding writers as I know very few poets who write about the Ahlulbayt (pbut) using the above structures.

It's very important when writing poetry regarding the Ahlulbayt (pbut), to understand that we are dealing with a topic of great emotional attachment, therefore it is easy for emotions to spill out into our writing. The problem with this is that if a poem does not have a centralised topic or theme it can lose its credibility as a poem.

This means that it is essential that we understand what we are setting out to write and portray before we write a poem. Jumping between multiple topics in a single poem can come off as jarring if there is not a justifiable connection between these topics. Hence there needs to be an apparent balance of topics or topic in the final poem.

Personally, I try to ensure that every poem I write is not similar to a poem I have written previously, even if the story or event or personality being discussed has been discussed before in a previous poem. This can be done by changing the angle we are looking at the subject or the way we are discussing it.

There are also a number of methods that assist us in ensuring that every poem we write is original and new. Originality in a poem is key, as the whole idea behind a poem is to capture and entice the reader's attention. One particular way is in the use of metaphors.

Metaphors are the power of the poem, and can either be used subtly, for example, in a line or a verse, or be the main crux of the poem. It is important to be creative with metaphors as this will assist you in your creativity as you write. An example of the use of metaphor below:

> The sky to the Earth bends... the moon here it descends
> Toward the Earth descends the moon, and it looks at the river
> I've torn the skies to come to you and bring those children water

The use of paradox is another way to ensure that a poem is original, paradox being the impossible choice of impossible decision. It has such an effect on the mind that it baffles the reader with regard to what to consider as reality, or what to consider as the greater importance.

For example, discussing the worth of sunrise versus the worth of sunset, or the worth of one great historic personality verses the worth of another historic personality. Of course, neither has a greater worth, and neither does the sunrise or sunset have greater value over the other: this is what makes a paradox and what makes the concept so effective.

Another important aspect of content is the chorus. It is important when writing a chorus to understand that the chorus must be what grabs the attention of the reader immediately, as it is the selling point of the entire poem. Also, it sets out the topic of the entire poem which the remainder must follow, although of course, it can expand and clarify whatever is stated in the chorus.

Finally, I wanted to share the various classes into which I have divided my poetry. Everything that I write can be classified with one of the following. I am including this as to promote ideas in aspiring poets and writers who are looking for ideas or inspiration.

1. The Ahlulbayt A-Z: Here, the poem aims to present multiple personalities of the Ahlulbayt (pbut) in a certain light. This can be for example, presenting Imams 1-12 and their virtues, or describing and comparing the tragedies of multiple figures of the holy household. Essentially, it seeks to present a glimpse of the Ahlulbayt (pbut) in their entirety in a short space of time.

2. The personification: This type of poem revolves around a personified object, giving the quality of humanity, speech and character to a lifeless object, e.g. the sun, moon, a river, a mountain, etc. Due to its

personification, figures and personalities in the poem can interact with it much like they interact with other personalities.

3.　The love letter: A poem that does not necessarily have to be a literal letter, but a conversation of a lover (the writer) speaking to his/her beloved (a divine or historic figure). This can also be vice-versa.

4.　The statement: This is a poem that seeks to act as a debate or a rebuttal regarding a concept, an idea or a belief. For example, a poem on the right of man, or the right of belief, or evidences proving the Muslim religion or Shi'i school of thought.

5.　The conversation: Not to be confused with 'the love letter', this depicts a conversation in history between two historic figures. It is important here to be intimate and romantic with words, looking at the relationship between the two personalities as well as their statuses. For example, a conversation between Imam Hussain (pbuh) and Ali Akbar (pbuh) should also focus on the idea that it is a con-versation between a father and son, etc.

6.　The biography: Similar to 'The Ahlulbayt A-Z', but instead it focuses on one individual personality, seeking to portray a biography of his/her life in poetic format. Of course, a literal biography would need volumes of books, so this is rather a glimpse into the life of a personality, but from his birth till his death, or else somewhere in-between.

7.　The scene: Here, there is no movement in terms of storyline, rather it discusses a specific scene or picture, poetically examining what we can see and feel. For example, a poem describing the battlefield of Karbala on the morning after Ashura.

There is much more to discuss with regard to mechanics behind the poetry that you will read in this book, but I wanted to explain these mechanics so that you have a greater understanding of how and why they are written the way that they are, hopefully adding to your experience. I also wanted to give an insight into how I write as I am often asked to do so by aspiring poets and writers, so I sincerely hope that the above was of use to you.

Reiterating what I have stated in previous books, this poetry is a part of me, my character, my spirituality and my heart, so I am truly honoured that you have chosen to read it. That which is written and left unread isn't lost, but that which is read is truly a blessing to the writer. So I thank you, and I pray that you find your journey through this book spiritually enlightening, educational and emotive.

Lastly, I pray that Allah (Subhanuhu wa Ta'ala) and the Ahlulbayt (pbut) accept this service from my humble hands, and that we are allowed to reach a stage where we consider Prophet Muhammad (peace and blessings be upon him and his family) to be our beginning, and Imam Mehdi (may Allah hasten his reappearance) to be our end.

Your servant,
Nouri Sardar

THE HOUSEHOLD CARVED IN GOLD

Poetry in memory of the holiest household

Everything has a beginning... and everything has an end
Muhammad is my beginning... and the Mehdi is my end"

Beginning & End
(In Celebration)

Everything has a beginning... and everything has an end
Mohammed is my beginning... and the Mehdi is my end
Between them is my existence... and it begins with the dawn
It ends when the sun departs and... blessings upon them I send

* * *

It did not start in a desert... rather, he began a light
Mohammed, the first creation... stole the gaze of Adam's eyes
From this began our beginning... the beauty of Adam's sight
And for his end at his own end... for Mehdi's return he cries
He lived a road that began then... with a sight that sparked his birth
Only when he'd welcome them all... was he content with demise
And twelve had followed Mohammed... and on such a road, he walked
He found it paved with divine gold... in each one a lesson lies

* * *

With Mohammed, something was born... beautiful until its end
He shaped the world for the better... setting the stage for them all
When it unveiled its curtains... I saw Ali after him
He taught me to only fear God... to rise whenever I fall
Then I remembered Mohammed... when I saw Hassan's patience
His name lit up this theatre... before his brother they'd call
I saw Hussain make his entrance... and it lasted till times end
He taught me if you seek justice... you can live an immortal

* * *

Some distance make this beginning... I saw the prayer of Sajjad
He who often recalled his end... in speech with his creator
And it was Baqir who taught me... of beginning and end
He built a university... upon it, as a teacher
He then passed his crown to Sadiq... a teacher's chair was his throne
He taught thinkers of modern Earth... as humanity's scholar
A crown Kathom wore imprisoned... he dipped it into patience
In prison he still captured hearts... guiding lover after lover

* * *

Ridha, they called him a stranger… but also called him a king
He who taught me to conquer hearts… with nothing but a smile
Referring back to beginnings… Jawad, he was but a youth
A youthful face on this roads end… taught me to grow up youthful
Hadi and Askari prepared… for the beginnings end
In the final act of this play… they guided the ungrateful
No-one wanted this play to end… so Mehdi prolonged his end
On those who know his beginning… he remains ever watchful

* * *

It's here that Adam still watches… fearful of turning away
For he who loved a beginning… must remain to watch the end
Enticed by the road that he walks… in love, the seconds prolong
The minutes attempt to stand still… simply to enjoy the trend
It is a love that not all know… not all remain till the end
And unless you complete this road… this house you won't comprehend
Mohammed was my beginning… it's something I won't forget
And left enticed by such a play… I'm still awaiting my end

BEGINNING & END

Everything Within Me
(In lamentation)

Everything within me... Haideri, Hussaini
I am... in every breath and every moment
I am... nothing except Ahlulbayt's servant

* * *

My life and death for me are but one and the same
I was drawn to them like a moth drawn to a flame
I did not care for my wishes, nor my own name
Everything that was mine, for this household became

I gave them everything... for a place on their wings
I am... patient, but for them I'm impatient
I am... nothing except Ahlulbayt's servant

* * *

I saw them as the crown upon my creation
And alone I boarded the ship of salvation
It set sail and within my contemplation
They became my every thought and every action

Salvation I boarded... and fate, it applauded
I am... in my smiles and my bereavement
I am... nothing except Ahlulbayt's servant

* * *

I saw, in two, divided the sons of Adam
I saw Ali alone and the world against him
I saw in awe of Zahra, even Maryam
And in my veins I saw blood of Bani Hashim

I made a decision... Ali and his children
I am... where I stand on the Day of Judgement
I am... nothing except Ahlulbayt's servant

* * *

I breathed in their love whilst everyone else would drown
My service to them became, on my head, a crown

And never, not once, could anyone put me down
When I had Ali's smile and Abbas's frown

All in me they would see... Haideri, Abbasi
I am... because of them, always triumphant
I am... nothing except Ahlulbayt's servant

* * *

How many from the cradle, this house they have seen?
Some were born to them but adopted I had been
Some were Fatima's sons, and for this they wore green
I wore black for I'm the son of Ummul Baneen

For Hussain, her children... and I am one of them
I am... to this house but a mere present
I am... nothing except Ahlulbayt's servant

* * *

A thorn, but with their love into a rose I grew
I had sins but they acted like they never knew
With their tales, their names into my heart they drew
Till every morning my love for them I'd renew

They never left my side... my comfort when I cried
I am... speechless if ever I am silent
I am... nothing except Ahlulbayt's servant

* * *

When it comes to the day I am fragile and old
I'll tie a belt just so Hussain's flag I can hold
In my last days if "you wasted your time" I'm told
I'll say everything's dust and only Ali's gold

Haideri till I die... Hussain's name in my eye
I am... till my last days and final moments
I am... nothing except Ahlulbayt's servant

* * *

My Greatest Deed
(In lamentation)

My years, they lie within your hands... my destiny beside you stands
In all that I read... in the blood that I bleed... you became my greatest deed

* * *

I speak to you in love's secrets... with tears that I hold
I wipe these tears into my eyes... my eyes I blindfold
With all the most beautiful names... my eyesight I scold
So that they only witness you... when it I unfold
I speak with a river of tears... that I can't withhold
Your love exists within each tear... I wake from its cold
I speak to you all of a love... that can't be controlled
All that I have, all that I am... to your house I sold
My years, they lie within your hands

A promise... I've made toward myself
A promise... for you, my age and wealth
A promise... that in sickness or health... my greatest deed

* * *

I've promised destiny for years... and my fate I've told
That even till my dying days... your house I'll uphold
Even if my age it withers... and I become old
I'll spend my last days in your service... toward your household
Uncontrollably, around you... my life I would mould
Whatever didn't grow to you... it I would remould
And in the love of your service... daily my heart strolled
I saw everything else as dust... and saw you as gold
My years, they lie within your hands

A promise... by the tears that would flow
A promise... by smiles and sorrow
A promise... that for you I would grow... my greatest deed

* * *

I accepted the chains of fate... my heart it patrolled
I sold my dreams to your wishes... that which was foretold

I had secrets only you knew… memories untold
Whilst all others were comforted… my wounds you consoled
Then I understood your beauties… into me you'd fold
And I raised my head with your love… infront of the world
When it came to serving your house… nothing I'd withhold
In poetry, I'd proclaim to all… this is them, behold

A promise… in all that I've written
A promise… that lives in my children
A promise… that to you I've given… my greatest deed

* * *

(London – 11/06/13)

Iraq's Shrines
(In lamentation)

Iraq your beauty each golden shrine defines
I'm missing the scent of your beautiful shrines

* * *

A memory and daily I yearn for her
Seeing Kadhom, the prince of Kadhemiya
Wishing a return, my wishes I gather
The sight of two domes within my pupil shines

* * *

My hopes shattered glass, I collect every shard
And present my years as a youth to Jawad
To gift toward he who beautifies Baghdad
For this city's beauty Jawad's hand designs

* * *

I miss Balad's scent and a sight my tears shed
In each tear I see Sayed Mohammed
Recalling his visit on the tears I'd tread
Adoring wishes coming true as his signs

* * *

I recall a dome whose voice screams to me pain
And cry "stay patient" to the Askeriayn
By his last abode, to Mehdi I complain
The last place he was seen, its painful confines

* * *

I ask myself why they saw it as worthless
By the Askeriayn, Sayeda Narjis
Beside two princes is a buried princess
Gifted by the Lord to the best of bloodlines

* * *

I yearn for a place, that its sight makes me weep
The sons of Muslim in Muslim's absence sleep
Drenched in tears of visitors that on them seep
They seek their father, their murderer declines

* * *

Every day from the mosque of Kufa I hear
The heart-wrenching call of Fajir's call to prayer
O' Mukhtar and Muslim, Ali's death is near
Ali's head with Ibn Muljim's sword aligns

* * *

It's presence a dream, a torture its absence
A kingdom where Ali, my crown, is its prince
Recalling his scent, which lover keeps patience?
The father of all, his golden shrine enshrines

* * *

Years after his death, his presence I feel
The generous Abbas, father of zeal
Return me to you, at your grave I'd kneel
My wishes I write, your generosity signs

* * *

My existence to a sole purpose returns
A mention of his name and him my heart yearns
When I hear "Hussain" to his grave my heart turns
And my invite to return Habib resigns

* * *

(London - 03/08/13)

Opening Verses II

Mohammed

I tell you that my first and last is Mohammed
And that all are one and the same Mohammed
Only God and one other perceive Mohammed
None knows Ali except his Lord and Mohammed
Mohammed's Ali and Ali is Mohammed
For only Mohammed can succeed Mohammed
It doesn't end there, forever lives Mohammed
The greatness in each, the greatness of Mohammed
Mohammed's Mehdi and Mehdi is Mohammed
For only Mohammed can conclude Mohammed
Mohammed began and ended Mohammed
Mohammed moved on and replaced him, Mohammed
And for this I send blessings upon Mohammed
Blessing him and the family of Mohammed

Twelver

Ask about my masters, they're nine and eleven
Twelve, with Ali: the peak of eloquence they begin
They continue with the peak of patience, Hassan
With Hussain they became youth's masters in Heaven
And Sajjad with prayers, the hearts to God he'd open
And Baqir who taught gold with words he had spoken
And Sadiq who fathered the school we reside in
And Kathom who with patience conquered his prison
As Ridha was pleased with whatever was written
And Jawad who with his youth would, old minds, weaken
And Hadi and Askari who, in eyes, glisten
Waiting for Mehdi to once again awaken
With all these names, a prayer upon my eyes written
Blessings on Mohammed and on his twelve children

I Really Don't Know

I really don't know just how your love reached me
Maybe it was from all the sayings I'd read
Or maybe it was awe from such a young age
From all the stories my father had said
Or maybe it was from my mother's own touch

And it reached me in the food to me she fed
Or was it something fused within my bloodstream
For it cried "Ali" whenever it was shed
Or maybe something deep in my nature
As with his name nothing I would fear or dread
As if it was made in the essence of me
With my creation, deep within me embed
I found proclaiming it was something I yearned
With the love of Ali, high I held my head
My tongue blessing him by blessing Mohammed
"O' Lord and the family of Mohammed"

Mathematics

I found so many flaws when from 1 to 3 I counted
They felt out of place, too light, by uncertainty tainted
I lost all faith in numbers, every number I hated
For I was counting through numbers on imbalance mounted
But I kept on counting, and by number 4 I was greeted
And I felt like number 1 on number 4 was weighted
I felt that this was number 1, the balance I awaited
I was overwhelmed by its power, I almost fainted
I knew it was number 1, all my life I've waited
For a number that as number 1 can be accepted

So if you accept Ali as number 1
And you accept what the Prophet has said
Let me hear you send all your blessings upon
Mohammed and the family of Mohammed

Salutations

Congratulations (or lamentations)
Salutations
Towards the
Best of creation;
Father of a nation

The king by whom we are led
The beat of the blood we've bled
The hand from which knowledge is fed
The saint who Khadija wed
He who God told "read" and read

Who sought comfort in God's stead
Who preached God till his deathbed
To thinkers, miles ahead
He who died but isn't dead
Who jewels rest in what he's said
The knower of the unsaid
To Islam's body its head
Whose teachings on which we tread
'Abul Qassim' (Al-Mustafa) Mohammed

Ali

Ali with his death, Qurans ascend
Ali with his birth, heavens descend
Ali the truth that others pretend
Ali, all ran yet he would defend
Ali till now to orphans he'd tend
Ali to Ali courage he'd lend
Ali - a "master", not a mere "friend"
Ali today, none comprehend
Ali, scales toward him bend
Ali the beginning that has no end
Ali the infinite, undying trend
Ali, blessings upon him we send

The Chain

A desert, with the vapour of sin, more humid
The vice of sin could not be more... amid
This sin the Lord descended Mohammed

He was truth embodied, he told not a lie
He was the sun that rose not late and not early
Who opposed him? Not Khadija, not Ali

Infact Ali held Badr and fought in her
He lifted the gate of Khayber's fort in her
If he did bleed, his wounds were wiped by Fatima

Fatima wouldn't leave his side and hasn't
Like the moon wouldn't conflict the sun and hasn't
She gave birth to both Hussain and Hassan

Killed by his wife, none would call her sane
None could see his enemy and say he's sane
Hassan stood, but with Yazid rose Hussain

The tyranny of Yazid his sword jarred
His glare shook evil, all evil he saw, jarred
His battle continued by Zainab and Sajad

Seeking to reform the nation of Mohammed

* * *

THE MASTER OF CREATION

Poetry in memory of the holy Prophet Mohammed (pbuh)

"In the eyes of God he surpassed creation
The minds of men he's left in contemplation
Around his words built nation after nation..."

BEGINNING & END

The Garden
(In Celebration)

If they think I'm misled... I show them Mohammed
Mohammed, Mohammed... Mohammed, Mohammed

* * *

I've walked in a world of love and lessons... and saw it, a heavenly garden
When daily through this garden I strolled... I found with lessons it was ridden
It taught me how to stroll in my world... it took away each doubt and burden
And when with sins my heart would harden... its scent would cause my heart to open
How much I adored such a garden... to my dismay, men it tried to burn
That which, in my heart would once blossom... they'd defame, and to flame, make it turn

* * *

Indeed they'd tried to burn this garden... hoping that elsewhere I would wander
Hoping that I'd forget its beauty... and no more, on its lessons, ponder
But how beautiful was this garden... for it had taught me how to answer
As part of such a beautiful faith... how proud was I to be a member
When mocked and defamed was my garden... morals it taught me, I'd remember
I'd reply, and not out of anger... I'd draw for them the last messenger

* * *

They portrayed him as if he misguides... I replied with morals he'd taught
They told me he preached battle and war... I drew them lessons for which he fought
To show them the beauty of this man... a flower from his garden I brought
I crushed it and drew with its juices... an image that millions have sought
I showed them the lessons he left us... that calmed souls that were left distraught

I showed them his patience, love and faith… and with such things, the world's gaze he's caught

* * *

I'd speak to mothers and I'd show them… that Heaven, it lies beneath their feet
I'd go to who greeted us with hatred… and with roses, these souls I'd greet
And he who was boiling with anger… I'd serve him water to soothe his heat
And the orphan who'd lost a parent… to my kindness and love, him I'd treat
And when asked where I'd found such lessons… I'd take their hand to Mohammed meet
I'd ask them to stroll in his garden… and I'd show them this garden's beauty

* * *

(London – 23/01/13)

This is Mohammed
(In Celebration)

This is Mohammed... this is Mohammed
Today every Prophet's told... this is Mohammed

* * *

The Lord brings forth Adam... and he watches in awe
The first human being... God's first creation saw
They prostrated to me... but this light I adore
To be of his servants... the great Lord I implore

If someone's misled... if someone's misled
I'll personally tell them... this is Mohammed

* * *

Noah disbands his ark... and tells every nation
Leave my ship and board him... the ship of salvation
I lived nine hundred years... few loved my religion
He'll live sixty three years... love him will creation

Of him I have read... of him I have read
Billions will follow him... this is Mohammed

* * *

Abraham celebrates... and thanks his creator
I've paved the way for him... and built him the Ka'ba
Indeed of the Arabs... they call me the father
But he'll father mankind... and build them a future

To him they'll be led... to him they'll be led
Orphans see him a father... this is Mohammed

* * *

Moses parts the red sea... yet approaches humble
Hearts will part for his words... break will every idol
I've performed miracles... he is a miracle
In the flame of Ahmed... how many will dwindle

For words that he's said… for words that he's said
They'll be drawn moths to a flame… this is Mohammed

* * *

Soulaymon leaves his throne… and closes his kingdom
To visit the true king… and learn from his wisdom
He gives him his army… everything, he gives him
The greatness of this man… this king cannot fathom

Even tears he's shed… even tears he's shed
Left in awe of his beauty… this is Mohammed

* * *

Jesus turns to the world… to all those that love me
Follow me to Mecca… and behind we'll pray
This is your Judaism… your Christianity
Alone, he'll change the world… and every eye it will see

To Mohammed head… to Mohammed head
And each Prophet follows him… this is Mohammed

* * *

(London – 23/01/13)

Unspoken
(In Celebration)

In the words of men, his greatness left unsaid
Mohammed O' Mohammed O' Mohammed

* * *

He cannot be encompassed by words spoken
How can words define words that souls awaken?
The power of speech from tongues he has taken
The beauty of gold left in words unspoken

Beyond all that's spoken, heard, written or read
Mohammed O' Mohammed O' Mohammed

* * *

In the eyes of God he surpassed creation
The minds of men he's left in contemplation
Around his words built nation after nation
He retaught thinkers with each word and action

A revolution in every heart he led
Mohammed O' Mohammed O' Mohammed

* * *

He grew in the depth of an ocean, a pearl
Now the hearts of billions around him whirl
In a sea of souls his values he would hurl
He extended his hand to whom he saw crawl

The father whose values to orphans he fed
Mohammed O' Mohammed O' Mohammed

* * *

Gifted because to all his gifts he'd offer
For he knew men without his gifts would suffer
He saved the lost, awaiting them from afar
Not a man feels from him distant or far

And souls yearned from his words when on them they tread
Mohammed O' Mohammed O' Mohammed

* * *

Defines Mohammed not a praise nor a speech
Yet we find even today his name we preach
Even if today Mohammed you beseech
He awaits your questions, so you he may teach

Unspoken yet spoken as living, not dead
Mohammed O' Mohammed O' Mohammed

* * *

(London – 29/01/13)

In Their Eyes
(In Celebration)

I present you the virtues of Muhammad
I'll show you how he left non-Muslims in awe
Those who didn't even believe in his book
The greatness of this man, from afar, they saw
You don't have to be Muslim to love this man
Nor to believe in the ideas that he bore
Just look at the words of the thinker, Ghandi
The Sir William Muir, the playwright, Bernard Shaw
They called him the bother; father and saviour
And "the treasure of wisdom", as Ghandi saw

They saw that truth and goodness he embodies
Can you find such virtues living in bodies?
His name, it lit a flame in hearts and bodies

Muhammad read Muhammad led
Muhammad fed the orphans who were us, thirsty for knowledge
He'd soothe the tears that from ignorance would pour
And just as the orphan adores its carer
We would look up to him, and him we'd adore
And I'll show you now what non-Muslims have written
Found in the time's pages that never away wore:

Muhammad, the man of truth and fidelity
Muhammad, who's strength did not come through war
Muhammad, successful on multiple levels
Muhammad, the voice from nature's own door
Muhammad founded a nation; a empire
A religion, one more and he's found four
Muhammad and I could keep quoting his praises
But tell me, of this man, need I saw more?

Muhammad brought,
Muhammad sought,
Muhammad taught,
Muhammad thought

Muhammad's a teacher,
Muhammad's a scholar,
Muhammad's a father,

Muhammad's a brother,
Muhammad's a thinker,
Muhammad's a leader,
Muhammad's a preacher,
Muhammad's a lover,
Muhammad's forever…

All in the words of those who do not believe
None saw one like Muhammad before

* * *

(London – 06/02/13)

One of a Kind
(In Celebration)

Every day I ask my Lord to send blessings… on the greatest of mankind
If they ask why, I tell them whilst man is man… Mohammed's one of a kind
If mankind's good deeds were placed on a letter… by his hand it would be signed
If man were placed on the side of a scale… him on the other you'd find

> Crowned by his Lord, the best of creation
> Brought a mercy against man's destruction
> The ship boarded by our own salvation
> Mohammed's one of a kind

Every day I ask my Lord to send blessings… upon the sight of the blind
And I find that the teachings of this Prophet… manifest into my mind
In it his name erupts into a garden… coloured for the colour-blind
Ridden with roses of lessons for all men… the saviour of humankind

> He became gardens of contemplation
> Blessing him itself became a nation
> Then I knew with no doubt and no question
> Mohammed's one of a kind

And I cry out glory to the Lord whose hand… the light of Ahmed designed

> What a character and what a being… Living
> One thousand years and yet in everything… Living

> Living in his teachings like an ocean
> His teachings still reach us with affection
> The name remembered in each affliction
> Mohammed's one of a kind

O' my Lord send blessings upon Mohammed… who is your blessings defined
And if they ask why daily I send blessings… Mohammed's one of a kind

* * *

(London - 08/02/14)

All That Rises
(In Lamentation)

Father all that rises must set… our days with the sunset bend
But tell me how a love like ours… can meet such a tragic end?
Love disappears… drowned in my tears

* * *

There exists a love… born before we're born
Love for Mohammed… on our hearts is worn
It sleeps in our blood… if from it we're torn
Left in your absence… forever we'd mourn

O' father how can such a love… so entrenched within our blood
Be torn away from this same blood? … I watch it down my cheeks flood
Your love appears… drowned in my tears

* * *

I feel the sun set… deep within my heart
As if from my days… O' father I part
Our love like a day… beautiful its start
And yet its sunset… tears this day apart
Our hearts were one O' my father… today one half was stolen
And by your absence, the other… is left shattered and broken
My heart, it tears… drowned in my tears

* * *

You became the best… of all creation
And your absence has… broken a nation
But I swear, their grief… and lamentation
Does not equal mine… or my affliction

If my grief were poured onto skies… I'd see seven skies shatter
And in your absence O' father… no sun or stars would matter
Creation hears… drowned in my tears

* * *

NOURI SARDAR

When I was little... left me, my mother
I had one parent... that was my father
If you left my sight... I'd would look further
If I'd not find you... this rose would wither

A rose planted upon this earth... searches for all it has known
The stem of those rose has been crushed... your absence upon it thrown
An orphan's fears... downed in my tears

* * *

Whatever begins... ends eventually
And there are deaths in... every family
But none have had you... you touch beautifully
Let all die, just leave.... Mohammed only

I wish the world would break in two... and take away everything
For it would be a better place... if only you were living
Born are my fears... drowned in my tears

* * *

I cry out a scream... come back Mohammed
For I see fire... to our house is led
And I see ashes... covering my head
From a nail's pierce... I see blood has bled

I feel torture none have felt... and toward your grave I turn
Along with my door and my heart... I watch my love for you burn
The fire nears... drowned in my tears

* * *

(London - 26/02/14)

THE PEAK OF ELOQUENCE

Poetry in memory of the Commander of the Faithful (pbuh)

"They tell me that my love for him left faith in division,
I tell them without this love there would be no religion..."

A Glimpse of Ali
(In Celebration)

The world listens when his name, with love, I utter
And I play with its awe when I speak of Haider

I speak of his virtues, the world drowns in silence
Yearning his stories, twitch the ears of the listener
I find myself standing, as the world watches me
I'm left in a paradox as Ali's writer
The virtues of Ali can't be confined to words
Can I describe his words, actions or his nature?
So I take a deep breath, and I swallow my fears
I speak the unspeakable love of the lover
I speak as the proud student of the greatest school
And feeds the ink of my words the greatest teacher

And just when I think that writing about him is impossible
He speaks to my mind, reminding me nothing's impossible
And he reassures my inspiration, saying, it's possible

To understand me through words, don't ask me why, it just is
Infinity can't be confined, but for me it just is
Because if words couldn't hold me, it wouldn't be justice

To the people I was sent to guide, for I am a motional
Quran that walks and talks and heeds and thinks and does, a motional
Beacon of love that guides hearts and leaves them for me, emotional

So I speak to you now the virtues of Ali
in war, feared by even the greatest warrior
In speech, his sentences, the peak of eloquence
His patience a wood invincible to fire
His charity known only by the dark of night
His prayer became the soul-mate of this worshipper
His justice embarrassed the straightest of scales
His wisdom would topple the greatest oppressor
Ali was the soldier, the leader, the trader
The teacher, preacher, the believer, the father

When faith was at the hands of the highest bidder
Ali was challenged by each and every bidder

And his sword left each of them buried in Badr

Thinking that Badr was a fluke, they faced him at Uhud
His sword smiled at their anger saying to them, I had
All of you at your heels at Badr, just like I had

Mercy on an army that we didn't face at Jendel
They robbed and thieved, but ran away when we came to Jendel
They feared me even when I was sheathed, harmless and gentle

Yet there came those who would have no knowledge of our conduct
Amr Ibn Wudd who has a strike that no-one can duck
Ali killed him, but still, left his gold and wealth at Khandak

For Ali didn't care for worldly things, at Khaybar
No-one could lift the gate, except for Ali, at Khaybar
Who does this when he only eats hardened bread? None can, bar

Ali, who never had pride, he wasn't a man insane
Even though many basked in their pride as though they're insane
Which is why many suffered but Ali won at Hunayn

And he won battle after battle, just like at Ta'if
The last battle he fought with Mohammed was at Ta'if
To usurp Ali's golden position none would try, if

Someone did, his army was cursed by Mohammed, so if seen
Was a sword raised against Ali they'd be cursed, and so if seen
Was Muawiya fighting Ali, he's cursed at Soffeen

Which shows that Ali's sword, gifted by God, was a gem, all
Swords of diamond, gold and silver jealous of this gem, all
Would see its justice and valour when he fought at Jamal

And every historian and observer would know he won
Every Islamic battle that he partook in, know he won
And he proved this with the last battle of his life, Nahrawaan

And in each battle he didn't just fight, he taught
Entering even the plains of battle a preacher
He would not strike Amr Ibn Wudd when angry
The greatest warrior, yet feared his own anger
He'd not let his sword kill a single human being

Were he to be a kind, good man in his future
He only fought in defence, and fought when attacked
He stood for justice against each unjust leader
A symbol of the free on the battlefield
He brought love to goodness and left evil in fear
On the battlefield, the lion of your Lord
Off the battlefield who knows who you are?
Ali, the voice of human justice for all men
Ali, who the greatest thinkers on him ponder
Ali, whose words are the peak of eloquence
Ali whose speech contains oceans of wonder
Ali, he who governed a third of today's world
Yet could not bear to see even a Christian poor
Ali and I could praise him till the end of times
And I'd still find lessons to delve in and explore

Ali
Ali's greatness, Ali's fairness, Ali's braveness
Ali's fearless, Ali's selfless, Ali's priceless
Ali's flawless, Ali's ageless, Ali's endless
Ali
Ali's wonder, Ali's grandeur, Ali's Badr, Ali's Haider
Ali's higher than every number one after him, immortal
Transcendent of time and of space is this figure
No, Ali can't be confined to any poem
But a glimpse of Ali can last for forever

* * *

(London – 03/11/12)

The Difference
(In Celebration)

They ask me the difference between hellfire and Heaven
I say between the left and right hands of Abel Hassan

* * *

They ask me about my Islam as if I don't believe
And they ask me such as if I'm anything but human
They ask me in a way where they demean my existence
And expect that I'll stutter and will answer with caution
They ask me in a way that they know all of the answers
I answer in a way that's more certain than they're certain
I answer them when they ask me why I "overpraise" him
Because he was born in the magnet of your prostration

* * *

They tell me that my love for him is strictly forbidden
I tell them forgetting his love is an innovation
They tell me that we make him to be something that he's not
I tell them if he's not great, why isn't he forgotten?
They call me a disbeliever and a polytheist
I say call me what you want, my faith is still unshaken
They tell me that my love for him left faith in division
I tell them without this love there would be no religion

* * *

I answer when they tell me that this love has made me mad
Then how is it I've used logic to reach this conclusion?
They ask me how is it you believe such insanity
I say I never kept quiet when I had a question
They tell me how can you say that he was meant to be first?
I tell them after three he was begged for that position
They say how can you choose him over those Mohammed loved
I say when others ran, he gave Mohammed protection

* * *

They say how can you choose him as first when they chose a first
I say the Lord chose my decision, not an election
They say Khaybar was all he did, don't pretend he did more
I say that the gate to Mohammed's city he'd open
They say how can you say he had a say in miracles?
I say only Ali can affect the sun's rotation
They say how can you say that Ali is just like the moon?
I say Mohammed's the sun, Ali is his reflection

* * *

They tell me I'm wrong and I'm destined for hellfire
I tell them I have Ali, my faith is never shaken
They tell me I lie, I tell them nothing have I hidden
You look into my eyes, you see "O' Ali" is written
You see the letters of his name in my pupil glisten
You see I've given him my soul, my house and my children
You see I've given him all that you have never given
And even if I'm wrong, I'll wait for his intercession

* * *

(London – 25/10/13)

BEGINNING & END

Your Sweet Name
(In Celebration)

In every moment… breathed in is your name
And sweeter than air… your name it became
Flowing deep within my veins… your name immortal remains

* * *

Ali on my tongue, and it did not find one sweeter than Ali
Ali, my heart flutters whenever my tongue's spoken Ali
Ali, and never has my tongue once forsaken Ali
Ali took the chains of my love and love's taken Ali
Ali in my words, and they seek to reawaken Ali

Ali drew me in when by my tongue he was praised
A lover's crush and, his name, it left my heart dazed
Every love your name it drains… your name immortal remains

* * *

Ali know I found that only love could comprehend Ali
Ali in the beat of my heart, daily it would trend Ali
Ali, if confused, my love would toward my heart send Ali
Ali, if my heart was wounded, my love it would lend Ali
Ali, if fallen, my love toward me would extend Ali

Ali, your name became the tune of my heartbeat
And daily my mornings would love of Ali greet
Upon my heart's barren plains… your name immortal remains

* * *

Ali became my pupil, therefore my eye just sees Ali
Ali beautified my sight, reminding me that he's Ali
Ali taught me to recall him and so death frees Ali
Ali's beauties in my eye, daily it studies Ali
Ali can only be known by saying Ali is Ali

Ali, worlds apart we stand and my eye searches
For the heavenly throne on which your name perches
And when this throne it attains… your name immortal remains

* * *

Ali, what a name, and how many, their children, name Ali
Ali on their foreheads, and with this their hearts became Ali
Ali's the picture that each house hangs up with the frame "Ali"
Ali's one, and all know there can never be the same Ali
Ali's love we can't be blamed for, for none would dare blame Ali

Ali, every house their household to you presents
Before they decide to, their love for you consents
Mortality, it complains… your name immortal remains

* * *

Ali found me an orphan, and an orphan I found Ali
Ali rejoiced at my voice and I adored the sound "Ali"
Ali crowned me a king, and my love for Ali crowned Ali
Ali drowned me in tears, but my tears have never drowned Ali
Ali circled my heart and my heart circled around Ali

Ali became a love that was like no other
His name fed to my cradle by my own mother
Time from him never refrains… your name immortal remains

* * *

Ali's a garden and daily I would wander Ali
Ali ponders my sins and my sins they all ponder Ali
Ali gave all to me, yet I'd not surrender Ali
Ali's my enemies' fear, and they'd never hinder Ali
Ali's just one, and my love did not find a splendour Ali

Ali, the name that my heart saw as immortal
I breathed his name till I became old and frail
Your name a cure to my pains… your name immortal remains

* * *

(London – 20/03/13)

My First is Ali
(In Celebration)

Who can put you fourth, really?   My first and my last is Ali

* * *

Firstly, let me tell you that as the first you're destined
I did not think for a second that you were second
Three letters and never as third have them I visioned
None can come forth and put you fourth till them I have questioned

You're the one who won my heart and like one we'd become
Two hearts into one soul and to me you would come
Three letters set me free, imprison me could no-one
Who'd make you four when forever, before all you're one

* * *

You won one and therefore I raise you from 4 to 1
And infront of the whole world I count 4, 3, 2, 1
With wonder full, how wonderful that like you is no-one?
I abbreviate your name, it becomes no dot one

Your name too long for two, it falls to one from two
If they put your name into it, then it breaks in two
If two gather together to make one they're still two
Let them bring all the numbers, they still won't equal you

* * *

I laugh when I see that of one, so jealous is three
Three letters as one and each one taught me to be free
Three magnificent letters, so how can four they be?
Only three letters can be one and they spell 'Ali'

For Ali, four is disgrace, he can't be four, ever
He can't be four when he's loved before four forever
His names' formations, they can form nations, each letter
'Ali' spells 1 and don't get me started on 'Haider'

* * *

A 1 in the middle of 'A', and two either side
The bottom of L's a 1, and on 1 it resides
And the 'I', well that's just a number 1 you can't hide
His name's made of 1's I can't make him 4 if I tried

And if I leave numbers and look at what you achieved
One soldier, one leader, one speaker, one Lord in you weaved
One born in the house of God, and in One you believed
He's unique, one, unlike anyone, don't be decieved

* * *

(Dearborn – 25/03/13)

BEGINNING & END

Do Not Hate Me
(In Celebration)

Don't forgive me... with his love I find repentance
Don't respect me... his love defeats my arrogance
Do not hate me... with his love, there is no patience...
Don't hate me for loving him

* * *

I dug and I discovered gold... 'til now I see its shine flicker
By its beauty I was bitten... at its memory I wither
A weight on me, but I don't care... I just wish it was heavier
And when the world sees me lift it... they'll see I'm in love with Haider

Do not judge me... by his love I have been bitten
Don't question me... three letters in my eye written
Don't pity me... everything else I've forgotten...
And I'm still thinking of him

* * *

Don't mistake envy for pity... don't look down on me for my crush
With Ali, all the hurt you see... I planted as a garden lush
You're tortured by words that chain you... I've become content with my hush
I walk a dreamer's paradise... where Ali's virtues to me rush

Don't convince me... I'm in love with this confusion
Don't return me... I love that he's in my vision
Don't capture me... I'm lost within my decision...
I love being lost with him

* * *

I stand on the highest mountain... I want every soul as my crowd
I've plummeted and my heart... to fall for Ali I've allowed
My eye sees him just like the sun... my heart circles him like a cloud
And upon the earth's highest peak... I raise my head with his love, proud

Don't challenge me... with Ali's love, all I've toppled
Don't attack me... I won when his love I wrestled
Don't offend me... for his love, the moon I grappled...

None come between me and him

* * *

With Ali you taste a sweetness… and its effects are addictive
You let all flutter in the wind… to his name your own soul you'd give
A love so strong that it stings you… on him you'll be contemplative
With this love I've conquered my soul… in the path of Haider I'll live

Don't define me… he's conquered my love and logic
Don't refine me… I love him, let it be tragic
Don't confine me… with Ali, I'll show you magic…
And you'll be in awe of him

* * *

(Toronto – 27/05/13)

Ali in 60 Seconds
(In Celebration)

His stories they leave minds in confusion
Minds cannot encompass him, can vision?

Ali's more than just Badr's victor
He's thirst for those who love to ponder
He's the mirror of his own mirror
The opener of doors since Khaybar

I knew him since my eye's first peek
I spoke him since I knew how to speak
Tears are embarrassed to stroll his cheek
He is eloquence, not just its peak

His virtues leave life's spirit breathless
63 years knew he was endless
Death understood his age is ageless
Immortal, he isn't worth less

In understanding him there's still confusion

* * *

(London – 12/08/13)

Martyred in Prayer
(In lamentation)

The victor of Badr... martyred within his prayer
In his final moments... the universe laments

* * *

I see the sun delay its ascent out of fear
Scared to see Ali's state when on Earth it'd peer
A night that seems much longer than it would appear
Begins to weep when a small sentence it would hear
Ali enters the mosque, within his eye a tear
"Get up Ibn Muljim, do not delay your prayer"

Rise and carry out fate... to my Lord I'll prostrate
To his death he consents... the universe laments

* * *

I see fate and what's written all in division
To change what's written I see trying, creation
Cries the dust that would once yearn his prostration
"My beloved pray elsewhere, lest you meet your doom"
The moon attempts to prolong its circulation
"How can I leave and rise tomorrow an orphan?"

Everything for him weeps... as fate upon him seeps
Undying bereavements... the universe laments

* * *

I see that your name brings the call to prayer its grace
You testify in one Lord and fate you embrace
You cup your ears for prayer, cries the Ka'ba you face
"Don't pray there O' Haider, return to your birthplace"
The sound of thunder to the Heavens I retrace
To bear the weight of Jibraeel's call, the worlds brace

Worlds toward Kufa tilt... to see if blood's been spilt
All scents become death's scents... the universe laments

* * *

Your gaze fixed upon God whilst all to you would turn
You yearn your Lord whilst Ali everything would yearn
You prostrate to your Lord whilst your cheeks, your tears burn
"How will I meet my Lord" is your only concern
In your fear, your final prostration you lengthen
"We belong to God, and to God we shall return"

You rise, his sword descends… its blade, your skull, bends
Poison in its remnants… the universe laments

* * *

Jibraeel's cry to beyond existence, it soared
And from the eyes of the uncreated, tears poured
Your head and your fast both broken by a poisoned sword
For breaking fast, apologetic to your Lord
Don't weep O' Haider, the seven Heavens applaud
And your throne in the highest Heaven is assured

Let your calamities… drown with all your worries
Your Lord Heaven presents… the universe laments

* * *

Tears in eyes burst just as the veins of your head burst
No man thinks of water, when for you is their thirst
The wielder of that sword, he prepares for the worst
You're Haider Ali, no man would blame an outburst
The father of Hassan killed within his fast
The martyr who offered his killer water first

"Offer this man water"… this is Haider Karrar
His soul your love torments… the universe laments

* * *

Anarchy in creation his death would create
Everything mourns Ali, every hour is late
I want you O' Ali's lover to contemplate
You who the love of Ali would, your life, dictate
Remember today when for Fajir you prostrate
Within that first prostration Ali met his fate

BEGINNING & END

Everything bids farewell… to the beloved that fell
His martyrdom torments… the universe laments

* * *

(London – 28/07/13)

All My Patience
(In lamentation)

All my patience... with my grievance
Falls apart within your absence

* * *

Today I bid farewell to all the good I've seen
My husband departs the arms of Ummul Baneen
I am torn between soothing my cries and between
Soothing the cries of Zainab, Hassan and Hussain

Roses wither... mountains falter
Gone is the world's sweetest fragrance

* * *

The gold for our marriage that once I would polish
I watch with the pillar of our house demolish
Could it be that to never have met you I wish?
Ali forgive me but I'm swallowed by anguish

Memories burn... for you I yearn
Missing your touch and your presence

* * *

They call me the mother of grief and of sorrow
What else would I become living in your shadow?
You plucked me a rose and within your hand I'd grow
Your death crushed this rose, down your hands, its blood would flow

I watch birds fall... broken, they crawl
Their wings broken by your silence

* * *

What began as a divine, holy lover's dream
Became a house of sorrow where only tears stream
Our marriage would once make the house of Ali gleam
My name in his heart, his name deep in my bloodstream

Destiny cries… what's written, dies
Lost in a weeper's ambience

* * *

Ali and in Ali are virtues like oceans
Ali and with Ali every secret opens
Ali and for Ali I raised for him lions
Ali without Ali his widow awakens

Rivers run dry… even stones cry
Defying logic and science

* * *

Ali and awaits Ali the throne of his Lord
Ali and came for Ali a heavenly sword
Ali descended Ali as God's written word
Ali, ascended Ali, the heavens applaud

Heaven's rejoice… left me no choice
But to mourn God's perfect guidance

* * *

To the pillar of religion I bid farewell
And alone soothe the cries of his children's wail
Descends upon our house angel after angel
And the legends of Ali toward them I tell

Even legend… grief cannot mend
History left in disturbance

* * *

(London – 21/07/13)

BEGINNING & END

The Sound of Thunder
(In lamentation)

Every creation of God hears the sound of thunder
The strike of a poisoned sword on the head of Haider
To the greatest father... farewell Ali Karrar

* * *

The sound of thunder, that rips apart the nightfall
His followers, in distress, toward his house crawl
How many men have been orphaned with his downfall?
Not the father of us, he's the father of all
Every man beneath the skies has heard thunder's call
With the strike upon Ali, Islam's pillars fall

Demolished Islam's pillars, and falls every pillar
Thunder strikes the foundations, they cry out for Haider
The voice of each pillar... farewell Ali Karrar

* * *

Chosen by God to the greatest person, succeed
Rises from prayer crying 'by God, now I succeed'
The battle-cry that not a soul would want to heed
Seeps from the head of Haider in blood that he'd bleed
He who can only be struck in the greatest deed
Cries out, "O' world, from your grip today I am freed"

The one who divorced this world embraces his slaughter
Saying goodbye to his house - his sons and his daughter
Their bereavements answer... farewell Ali Karrar

* * *

Upon Haider weeps the dust of which he fathered
Every rose that grew by his hand has now withered
By the house of Ali his lovers all gathered
Refusing to leave, their hearts to his bed tethered
Left in his blood, the head of Badr is shattered
The lion of God by Satan has been martyred

Upon the house of Ali, weeping are seven skies
Every thunder is a scream, its lightning is its cries
Every sky would falter… farewell Ali Karrar

* * *

The strike of Ibn Muljim, Ali had foretold
But wouldn't trade his prayer for more days in this world
This strike was vengeance against him for each household
That had a son whose soul to Ali's sword had sold
Ibn Muljim's sword the head of Ali had told
Did you not know that you are dust, and Ali is gold?

Within the mosque of Kufa, there was an explosion
With flowing blood arose the father of a nation
Upon him, left a scar… farewell Ali Karrar

* * *

His orphans cradle him, and cries every lover
O' children of Ali, to us he's a father
To hold the reigns of justice, none was worthier
The scale of justice, it bends towards Haider
"Where is our helper?" cries out the widowed mother
For the one who'd give him food, searches the beggar

His children saw the whole world when they're door they opened
Not just the house of Ali, the whole world is orphaned
Cries out the wide and far… farewell Ali Karrar

* * *

Najaf's dust rejoices in welcoming Ali
Hassan and Hussain leave Ali to its mercy
Under a moonless night, their father they bury
They lower him, Adam and Nuh take his body
Whatever truth Ali was, becomes legendary
In his grave, the words "ask me before you lose me"

Has the world ever witnessed a killed, murdered lion?
Not just Kufa mourns his death, but all of creation
Gone, his final hour… farewell Ali Karrar

BEGINNING & END

* * *

(London – 06/07/13)

When the Body Dies
(In lamentation)

In our eyes it is written... we are all Ali's children
And when the body, it dies... for Ali the heart it cries... we are all Ali's children

* * *

O' Haider we're your children... and in your name I begin...
To tell you of death O' Karrar
Whenever death calls our name... just like when to you we came...
We yearn for you as our saviour
For you we've lived and we've died... just like in life, we relied...
On you as our guide and helper
When death takes us, intercede... let the angels on us read...
That Haider is our hereafter
Whenever we had a wish... or drowned within our anguish...
We called for our intercessor
When into our sins we drown... turns into a golden crown...
The love for Mohammed's brother

Your love crowned our existence... our death seeks your assistance
On you, the soul, it relies... for Ali the heart it cries... we are all Ali's children

* * *

O' Haider in life you're hope... when climbing the steepest slope...
We call your name to be stronger
Your name, it brings such a strength... that no road is long in length...
It tells us to give up, never
When across mountains we crawl... or from mountain's peaks we fall...
When it is our darkest hour
O' Haider it's in our blood... that we call for our beloved...
You never fail to answer
We were taught from our cradles... the Ali brings miracles...
And teach the son would the mother
Haider's the father of dust... your wishes to him entrust...
He loves every son and daughter

The father of dust we'd call... knowing he's father of all

Just as our tears his hand dries… for Ali the heart it cries… we are all Ali's children

* * *

O' Haider we have a pride… and in this pride we reside…
It's in each servant and lover
That Haider as first we chose… for you the world we'd oppose…
O' Haider it is an honour
Our cradles could not deny… we're born with our heads held high…
A blessing from our Creator
Ali's name on our foreheads… Haider's in the soul embeds…
A pride that no-one could hinder
In the heart your flag it flies… every evil it defies…
And none can tear down its banner
From cradle until our death… from the first to the last breath…
"Ali's the only successor"

This pride is fused in our blood… it transcends all that we've loved
Till death as a flag it flies… for Ali the heart it cries… we are all Ali's children

* * *

A love that burns like a flame… fuels it, their envy and blame…
Never does it fall or falter
Is it our fault he's held dear… to blame Haider, none would dare…
When in one hand he held Badr
Would it be that for this oath… from every corner of Earth…
I'm labelled a "disbeliever"?
Regardless, they've understood… if alone on Earth I stood…
My belief won't fall nor wither
Give me in one hand, the world… the other, limitless gold…
And by God I would choose neither
Nothing challenges the worth… of a love I've had since birth…
And nothing can come close either

The world's aware of my place… it's tattooed upon my face
And in death with it I'll rise… for Ali, the heart it cries… we are all Ali's children

* * *

BEGINNING & END

O' Haider I have a dream… and it flows in my bloodstream…
in every grief, I remember
I recall a golden dome… and beneath it, lies the home…
Of the prince of each believer
With death's embrace, know I wish… in that moment of anguish…
I'd recall a moment tender
Standing alone at your door… with my eye, you, I adore…
An orphan beside his father
O' Haider in death's moments… a picture my mind presents…
Best said by the pen of Jaber

"When will I see your distress… by your door in my sadness…
I've missed seeing you O' Haider"

In death, it's drawn on my eyes… seeing you with my demise
And what a greater demise… for Ali, the heart it cries… we are all Ali's children

* * *

(London – 19/08/13)

With His Final Breath
(In lamentation)

Every believer, every lover of Ali at death
Is met by Ali, and his family with his last breath
His family for him cry... he sees Ali in his eye... with his final breath

* * *

Each lover and follower, if in Ali he believed
Is met by Ali, when his final breath this lover breathed
If the world tried to deceive him, but the world he deceived
Death is but another path for him and by death he's freed
If he served Ali and for Ali's tragedy he grieved
Visits him Ali and his family when he's buried

His eye it closes and approaches before him a light
His life was Ali, therefore Ali eases his own plight
Ali he didn't deny... he sees Ali in his eye... with his final breath

* * *

Be young or old, if from Ali he listened and he learned
Then seeing Ali, with his final breath this lover earned
Ali appears in the eye that for Ali's sight had yearend
When death you welcomed, your life you left, and to me you turned
Don't worry O' child of those who upon you have mourned
Concerned me your tears, now with your smiles, I am concerned

You believed in me, when all left me and I was alone
Now you are alone, to you I come, your deeds to me shown
Do not worry how and why... he sees Ali in his eye... with his final breath

* * *

O' child I know of your sorrow and of all your pain
Death isn't easy, but tragedy with you won't remain
If you died with my love, then in my eyes, you were slain
Welcomes you all those that for me martyrdom would attain
I'll shield you from all the tears that upon your grave rain
And for your service, I've brought with me Hassan and Hussain

Hassan he smiles, Hussain welcomes you with open arms
We welcome you and we place your palms into our own palms
For every tear, every sigh… he sees Ali in his eye… with his final breath

* * *

I have been gifted as the divide for heaven and hell
O' my follower, never does my lover in hell dwell
The fires of hell, if they call you, my Lord I shall tell
And of your service, at Heaven's gate, I'll quote and retell
Get up O' child, your family, bid them all farewell
Awaits you Heaven, and I'll ensure Heaven's scent you smell

Your sins forgiven, I have written your name with my own
Heaven awaits you, from me the angels your name have known
Your family bid goodbye… he sees Ali in his eye… with his final breath

* * *

They pulled your soul from your body and toward you I came
The pangs of death that all others fear, sweet for you became
I was waiting and Fatima mentioned to me your name
I am his mother, as you done for me, do him the same
O' child I buried her, and my wails none would tame
She saw me crying, but when she died toward her I came

When I left her grave, for me she'd crave, and then her eyes saw
When left had Ali, come had Ali, and she watched in awe
Just as when, there she would lie… he sees Ali in his eye… with his final breath

* * *

O' child take it from me, I know death isn't easy
But when I approach to my lover, easy it shall be
Even when I died, and all had cried for my tragedy
I opened my eyes and I saw that welcomed me had me
When I was lowered into my grave, Ali they'd bury
Ali had died, but I saw that welcomed me had Ali

I'm the supporter of my lover, even if it's me
Ali was my pride, therefore my Lord sent to me Ali

BEGINNING & END

The pangs of death he'd untie… he sees Ali in his eye… with his final breath

* * *

(London – 16/12/12)

BEGINNING & END

Sons of Ali & Hussain
(In lamentation)

Our mothers fed us a pride... sons of Ali and Hussain

* * *

O' he who speaks of our roots... understand our origin
Your roots lost in history... our roots are Bani Hashim
Virtue flows within our blood... the pride of Ali's children
We are enriched by our blood... golden within every vein

* * *

Virtues, if you understood... at our existence you'd kneel
Courage; valour; honour; pride... generosity and zeal
Fortitude; faith; selflessness... with sincerity we seal
You're a stain on history... history's crown we remain

* * *

Do not turn your eye to us... enemies know of our glare
Know when we sit, we kneel... to defend all, we prepare
Do not force us to spring up... fuel our anger, do not dare
If we had sold our patience... to us households would complain

* * *

Our mothers fed us tales... of Uhud and of Badr
Your forefathers ran away... remained, our father Haider
They wanted Muhammad killed... defended him, our leader
We are the sons of Ali... we defend Muhammad's reign

* * *

Our mothers fed us tales... rivers of tears, our eyes shed
In these rivers we evolved... in a legacy we'd tread
Of the father of freedom... the grandson of Muhammad
We became lost in Hussain... a love no-one could explain

* * *

Our mothers fed us a pride… from our cradles, it we'd see
We found an identity… and grew up at its mercy
Haideri and Husseini… Fatimi and Abbasi
However much it burns you… from this pride we won't restrain

* * *

(London – 11/05/13)

BEGINNING & END

Najaf
(In lamentation)

I came to Najaf in searching of the prince
For too long tortured me has Ali's absence

* * *

I came to the land of zeal and honour
The kingdom where Ali's the king and leader
Where each man says in pride, "my prince is Haider"
And all are in awe of Ali's brilliance

* * *

I returned missing the scent of Najaf's dust
Air that quenches the lover of Ali's thirst
The thirst to see Ali, into tears I burst
How long I've longed for my beloved's presence

* * *

I came greeted as if I was family
As the tears in my eyes cry out "finally!"
A stranger welcomed by the sons of Ali
Najaf perfumed me within Ali's fragrance

* * *

I came bringing the tears within which I'd drowned
I've walked in a desert and water I've found
I was a servant, now a king I've been crowned
Lost, but with the prince Ali I found guidance

* * *

Broken, I stood alone at the lion's door
The prince of believers my eye would adore
And in the love of Ali my tears would pour
I'd speak to my beloved in words of silence

* * *

You're in my heart, but from my eyes you're absent
My eyes dream of seeing your grave and lament
When in Najaf, I cherish every moment
For when I leave Ali, tortures me, patience

* * *

(London – 29/04/13)

I Ask You By Ali
(In lamentation)

Tonight destiny I defy... by telling God: I ask you by
Ali Ali Ali Ali

* * *

With three letters, my Lord I plead
By the blood this night he would bleed
Just as you cried, and all would heed
With your name, Ali, "I succeed"

I feel the tears of grief dry... by telling God: I ask you by
Ali Ali Ali Ali

* * *

On this night O' Haider listen
With your name I'll change what's written
I'd say a thousand times, not ten
"By Ali", and watch doors open

If anyone asks how or why: by telling God, I ask you by,
Ali, Ali, Ali, Ali

* * *

Ali, your name a lover's dream
And it flows fused in my bloodstream
It comforts my eyes when tears stream
With it, nothing difficult seems

From me, I see destiny shy... by telling God, I ask you by:
Ali, Ali, Ali, Ali

* * *

Born in the greatest location
On Friday, day of religion
Struck in the greatest position
Killed in the month of devotion

Can this man any prayer deny?   By telling God - I ask you by:
Ali, Ali, Ali, Ali

* * *

If ever, bled from me, a wound
I'd find it to your name attuned
Its pain with your name it perfumed
And with your name, Ali, it bloomed

Constantly it would soothe its cry... by telling God, I ask you by:
Ali, Ali, Ali, Ali

* * *

Ali I don't fear tragedy
Nor whatever's written for me
If ever looms calamity
I just cry "I plead O' Ali"

Fortitude on my neck I tie... by telling God, I ask you by:
Ali Ali Ali Ali

* * *

(London - 10/08/03)

BEGINNING & END

By the Son of Ali
(In lamentation)

With no family… he calls out proudly
"If I had a thousand sons I'd name them all Ali"
By the son of Ali… we'll never leave Ali

* * *

By our guide Mohammed who never told a lie
By the tears for his grandson that on the eye lie
By the household that never once uttered "I lie"
By the awaited saviour to whom we ally
By these moons never late and suns never early
Not a lie, on our eyes lies "allied to Ali"

The eye never lies… written on our eyes
We'll never leave Ali even if every eye dies
To prove we're with Ali… we swear it by Ali

* * *

Against seventy thousand he cried out "Haider"
A pride that slept in his blood and none could hide her
Against the world he held the pride of his leader
Against the seven skies like a flash of thunder
He replied when they cried "we shall avenge Badr"
"Ali is my leader and none could be prouder"

He killed thirty-five… for vengeance they'd strive
And yet one thousand years later, Ali's still alive
Always living, Ali… none can defeat Ali

* * *

His allegiance is not choice, it flows in the blood
All created from mud, but us from Ali's mud
The father of dust became to dust a beloved
And turned every grain of dust into a rose bud
The eye's gaze stays fixed on whatever the eye's loved
And against the shore of Ali his lovers flood

Just like skin and hair… or breathing and air

His name is fused with our blood and comforts all despair
In the bloodstream, Ali… unseperable, Ali

* * *

To Hussain his father was not just a parent
Their connection a secret and not apparent
If Ali was the perfume, Hussain was the scent
If Ali's the memory, Hussain's the moment
Against the world with Ali he was defiant
Just as we've held onto Ali despite torment

He saw Ali's worth… and cried with our birth
"We are with Ali if against the turn of the Earth"
When all hated Ali… we stood beside Ali

* * *

Seeing the strike on the head of Ali Akbar
Hussain remembers the strike upon his father
Like the strike on his father yet like no other
The strike does not reach his skull but reaches further
To the name 'Ali' no other was worthier
They wanted to kill Ali and found another

And all Hussain sees… are the two Alis
Two memories clash together like the clash of seas
The son he'd named Ali… had become like Ali

* * *

From the love of his father, daily, he would sip
"Ali" on his tongue and "Ali" upon each lip
Against the sea of enemies like a warship
He cries out "remembering Ali is worship"
Seeking Ali's love, arrows into his chest rip
Till the ship of salvation boarded Ali's ship

And still this Hussain… on Karbala's plain
Cries out "Ali's in my heart, my soul and every vein"
Headless, he meets Ali… in the love of Ali
* * *
(London - 17/02/14)

BEGINNING & END

Ali's My First Imam
(In lamentation)

In my eyes its written... no doubt and no division... Ali's my first Imam
The way the world defines me... a follower of Ali... Ali's my first Imam

* * *

Following Ali by God isn't a choice, it's a thirst
Thirsty we become when they say "fourth", we answer "he's first"
Glory to the One who doesn't let hearts from his love burst
Glory to He who gave us his love from first breath till last

Glory be to the Lord... who placed a heavenly sword... firmly in Ali's palm
With pride this sword we carry... a follower of Ali... Ali's my first Imam

* * *

Even if a sword reaches my neck and my life's taken
I'll only follow he who by God's own hand was chosen
Eyes are windows to the soul and in mine you see written
I am a Shi'a, son of Shi'a, Shi'a my children

"Ali" in allegiance... "Shi'i" in my existence... a pride that none can harm
Written with my destiny... a follower of Ali... Ali's my first Imam

* * *

Our belief in Ali never dies and never burns out
It's not even choice, it's in our blood, with no ounce of doubt
He represents us and yet his greatness few know about
What sprinkles in us overflows in him, even in drought

An image in our eyes... and history never lies... Mohammed raised his arm
I was taught my history... a follower of Ali... Ali's my first Imam

* * *

God made us obediant to him when us he designed
You'll find us wherever Ali and his children you find
Even if we find ourselves against the whole of mankind
We hear his name if we're deaf and see his name if we're blind

God told our destiny… salute the name of Ali… the greatest type of charm
Created intimately… a follower of Ali… Ali's my first Imam

* * *

It's not just Mohammed or Ali, it's their family
They father the orphan and they look after the lonely
They're not just a household of gold, they're divine and holy
We've seen miracles by crying out "help us O' Ali"

Ali brings miracles… beats his name and syllables… the pulse in our forearm
For Mohammed's family… a follower of Ali… Ali's my first Imam

* * *

To the knowing you as first after Mohammed we were born
When God first created us He'd see for Hussain we'd mourn
We made two promises and from neither can we be torn
We've sworn to follow you and to mourn your son we have sworn

The mourning of your son… like following you is done… a weapon none disarm
Haideri and Hussaini… follower of Ali… Ali's my first Imam

* * *

(London - 03/04/14)

THE LADY OF LIGHT

Poetry in memory of the leader of women of all worlds (pbuh)

"What fell, even thunder was embarrassed from its sound
What is worth so much that when it fell it hurt the ground?"

I Am Muslim

(In lamentation)

I am, no matter what they have said... Muslim
I believe in God and Mohammed... Muslim
Even if tears for Zahra I shed... Muslim

* * *

In the oneness of God, my faith, it testifies
And the love of Mohammed beneath my heart lies
The urge to disbelief, my soul, proudly defies
And it won't change if for Fatima my eye cries

How much we're told that we disbelieve... Shia
Because in our hardship we believe... Shia
Disbelief comes if Zahra we leave... Muslim

* * *

There exists, on Earth, a heavenly scent each year
It comes when a lover of Zahra sheds a tear
How easily the word 'disbelief' is thrown here
When tears are shed for Fatima, angels appear

Indeed with them, we remain content... our tears
We bathe within them when we lament... our tears
Tears that need only the Lord's consent... Muslim

* * *

How much we are told to stay hushed and be silent
Every year we show that our tears are defiant
Nor are we hushed of her tears or of her torment
Unlike those who from her funeral were absent

Indeed it exists with every cry... patience
But not when tyranny we defy... patience
We are, even if our tears don't dry... Muslim

* * *

Know that the love of this woman's universal
It is not only Shia, she inspires all
I ask how can mourning of her be immoral
When from her we take every lesson and moral

It's her we're following when we mourn… Zahra
And just like her, her grief we adorn… Zahra
Why not follow her if you were born… Muslim

* * *

I want the world to see the love of Mohammed
It flows in the tears that for his daughter he shed
If Fatima's from him and she is from Ahmed
Then every tear for her by Mohammed is read

Know that he collects them in his hands… Ahmed
And with those who sheds these tears he stands… Ahmed
He who loves Mohammed understands… Muslim

* * *

Is it a crime that I am showing you a crime?
You've taken me out of a faith I see sublime
You say disbelief with her name, time after time
How much disbelief you've uttered in your lifetime

Don't throw it around so casually… this word
Don't use it against love you envy… this word
If I accept her, I'm already… Muslim

* * *

From my cradle I saw that truth was with Haider
The love of Bani Hashim fed by my mother
When I hear the tale of the door and fire
My heart breaks for the tragedy of Fatima

Only the special call Fatima… mother
She is, if you're in love with Haider… mother
Only one name for all his lovers… Muslim

* * *

(London – 27/02/13)

BEGINNING & END

In Her Grave
(In lamentation)

He buries her... and he leaves her... in her grave, Zahra wants Haider

* * *

Alone, and to it no stranger... she sleeps, a bundle of roses
Shrouded by darkness of her grave... for her husband, Zahra searches
She sees a light above the ground... and Ali she recognizes
She calls his name without a thought... he does not hear, her grave she leaves

She calls his name... he walks away... and her cries, he does not answer
In her grave Zahra wants Haider

* * *

Left in the darkness of her grave... every memory, she'd recall
They rise above her like roses... and like arrows, on her they fall
When once, this lion would not sleep... if but a wound on her befell
She calls out his name in her pain... he does not come to soothe her call

She lies broken... with wounds ridden... silent remains Badr's victor
In her grave Zahra wants Haider

* * *

Trying to soothe her bleeding wounds... this broken rose turns to her side
She cries a sudden scream of pain... on her broken rib she resides
Not a soul comes to comfort her... no lion and none of her pride
And she's taunted by a fetus... a voice that comes from her insides

You're crushing me... mother, save me... let me live to see my mother
In her grave Zahra wants Haider

* * *

A woman with broken petals... yearns for the sight of her husband
She has not seen him for so long... and hurts Zahra, every second

85

Could it be that he does not come... when my absence to him's mentioned
O' Lord just let me hear his voice... with Ali's absence I'm burdened
In his absence... Ali's silence... becomes like her rib, her torture
In her grave Zahra wants Haider

* * *

You taught me, O' Ali, in life... to cry your name with each burden
I've cried your name, here in my death... how many times, but you don't come
You serve the neighbour and the poor... this is your wife, with wounds ridden
When I see you, welcomes me joy... my joy's left me with grief alone
I cried your name... no Ali came... I rest in my grave, a stranger
In her grave Zahra wants Haider

* * *

I do not mind if you forget... the moments where I made you smile
Or if you see the good I did... as unimportant or little
But O' Haider, would you dare bear... the pain of hearing me wail?
Come and visit me in my grave... heal the wound of the nail
Come and heal... pain I feel... my grave treats me as a stranger
In her grave Zahra wants Haider

* * *

She watches Ali leave her grave... and upset, Fatima becomes
Alone, tormented by her wounds... she lies a mother without sons
But when he leaves, she sees a light... it lights her grave, to her it comes
Ali he leaves, but in her grave... his beloved, Ali welcomes
He lights her tomb... and soothes her wounds... till time's end they are together
In her grave Zahra wants Haider

* * *

(London – 20/01/03)

Remembered
(In lamentation)

How many have suffered like I have suffered?
For years my tragedy will be remembered

* * *

In a cage of suffering I met my plight
And with my tears, a message of grief I write
Its ink overflows with the tears of my sight
Seeing my crushed child and house set alight
Flames that ignited my sorrows with its light
If they were poured onto days, they'd become night

To an ocean of sorrows I surrendered
For years my tragedy will be remembered

* * *

Muhammad, with my tears, Ali would bury
What some saw as death, I saw a tragedy
I surrendered myself to his soul's beauty
And embraced his death as a calamity
My tears filled a wound that his death left empty
I was a part of him, him a part of me

I used to cry his name and no-one answered
For years my tragedy will be remembered

* * *

Wandering the Lord of the world an orphan
Two weight things from Fatima they'd stolen
The inheritance of my father taken
And my husband's right to lead Ahmed's nation
To a world of injustice we'd awaken
It lay scattered with the graves of my children

A world of murder and hatred we'd entered

For years my tragedy will be remembered

* * *

At the house that angels visit, they gathered
No care for the house that Muhammad had fathered
Where even Satan toward us surrendered
They burned the house of the man that I mothered
The heavenly rose that Muhammad nurtured
They struck it, broke its rib and left it withered

And with a broken rib, alone, I wandered
For years my tragedy will be remembered

* * *

Hated by the world, I told the world, goodbye
O' Fitha don't tell my children that I'll die
I passed away and saw Hassan in my eye
Holding Hussain, uncontrollably he'd cry
And upon my chest for hours, they would lie
"O' mother get up and to our cries reply"

I watched the orphans that I had once mothered
For years my tragedy will be remembered

* * *

(London – 01/03/13)

The Tragedy of Fatima Zahra
(In lamentation)

This is the story that's written in time
Of our mother and against her a crime
This is the tragedy of Fatima Zahra... this is the tragedy of Fatima Zahra

* * *

This mother... let me tell you what once befell this mother
They'd smother... the unborn child within her, they'd smother
They'd smother... they'd smother, take him away from this mother
This mother... left to rock an empty cradle this mother
The love of her heart, from her womb taken
A blossomed womb became cold and barren
She felt and saw this child fall from within her... this is the tragedy of Fatima Zahra

* * *

A part... Muhammad's part of her, of him she's a part
Apart... after his death, she felt from his worlds apart
Apart... she complains to his grave how she's torn apart
A part... and a part of her desires her murder
She longs for her death as she longs for him
She sits there daily and sings him a hymn How much they oppressed me after you O' father... this is the tragedy of Fatima Zahra

* * *

Set of light... the house of Fatima was a set of light
Set alight... the house angels visited was set alight
Sat, a light... the house in which she prayed and she sat, a light
Set alight... set alight, in the flames she called for Haider

The house to which a thousand angels turned
She stood by the door as, in flames, it burned
She calls for Ali and she calls for her father... this is the tragedy of Fatima Zahra

* * *

I don't dye... do not ask me why my grey beard I don't dye

I don't die… when I buried her, I asked, why I don't die?
I don't die… when I recall her I ask, why I don't die?
I don't die… I long for my death just so I can see her

I see my own death as my happiness
Because I recall, her presence was bliss
If there is no Zahra, how can there be Haider? … this is the tragedy of Fatima Zahra

* * *

(London – 01/03/13)

Tonight

(In lamentation)

O' Zahra… O' Zahra

* * *

Tonight from every eye, tears of blood, for you fall
Every eye sees you crushed between the door and wall
Weeps for this sight, Zahra, the moon, the stars and all
And, with them, from a wounded heart, your name we call

* * *

Fire to the house that angels visit is brought
They tell him she's inside, and he shouts out "so what?"
With the blood of Zahra, the pledge of Ali sought
Between the door and nail Heaven's scent is caught

* * *

Crushed, the rose that brought joy to eyes of Mohammed
Ripped its petals, that flow in tears that his eye shed
His unborn grandson Mohsin to the nail led
And on his daughter the feet of oppressors tread

* * *

Bleeding from her chest, to Mohsin, she bids goodbye
"In the depths of my heart, child, you'll always lie
I'll see you a youth, not an unborn, in my eye
And to your grave daily I'll sing a lullaby"

* * *

Ali buries Zahra in the night, all alone
O' joy of my heart, by death from me you're taken
His hand feels the rib in her chest, it's broken
And the lion cries, a child left an orphan

* * *

(London – 20/02/13)

Another Day
(In lamentation)

How much we pray to see you... how much we pray
Another day it becomes... another day
It becomes light... it becomes night... and Fatima's still crying

* * *

How much we're told of your return... and how much we're left yearning
We raise our hands with the sun's rise... but the night leaves us bleeding
We begin every day with hope... and how we wake up smiling
But the night comes, we're left in awe... hearing Fatima crying

Who'll dry her tears, O' Mehdi... who'll dry her tears?
Days became years after this... days became years
She's our mother... and we ask her... when is your son returning?
It becomes light... it becomes night... and Fatima's still crying

* * *

How the lover seeks out his love... and tortured by their absence
We'd think you stood there at our door... but opened it to patience
Patience would become our torture... for us a lover's guidance
We'd leave our roses to flutter... in the wind of your distance

Love's impatient O' beloved... love's impatient
Why stay absent, just return... why stay absent?
Every heart-beat... it yearns to greet... the love of which it's dreaming
It becomes light... it becomes night... and Fatima's still crying

* * *

Every day Medina complains... of being struck by her tears
And its complaints, the world echoes... drowning in a sea of fears
She cries in the house of sorrows... every so often she peers
She yearns to see the sun rising... but only the moon appears

Tear down this moon with your hand... tear down this moon
Show us her tomb, assist her... show us her tomb

You disappeared... no-one appeared... to her no-one is coming
It becomes light... it becomes night... and Fatima's still crying

* * *

Do you not hear, daily, a call... from every edge of the Earth
It begins before the sun's rise... and continuous with its birth
You have a world awaiting you... how many know of your worth?
Why do you wait, when you're called gold... by nothing but dust and earth

Where is our gold, they all ask... where is our gold?
Pebbles we hold – our patience... pebbles we hold
Slowly dying... as she's crying... and with us she is dying
It becomes light... it becomes night... and Fatima's still crying

* * *

With all who weep for your absence... there are those who benefit
Just turn your eye toward Qunfudh... your mother, Zahra, he hit
With them the door and the nail... of the house angels visit
How many wish, that his mother... Imam Mehdi would forget

Don't forget her, Fatima... don't forget her
Rise, avenge her, O' Imam... rise, avenge her
Every second... for you beckons... to come out from your hiding
It becomes light... it becomes night... and Fatima's still crying

* * *

We united in the mourning... of your mother's tragedy
We began yearning the return... of the grandson of Ali
We began counting the seconds... hearing her calamity
And with Zahra, we raised our hands... O' Lord return him to me

Return Mehdi back to us... return Mehdi
Eyes want to see our saviour... eyes want to see
No more patience... no more absence... and not a day of waiting
It becomes light... it becomes night... and Fatima's still crying

* * *

(London – 17/02/13)

Piece of Heaven
(In Celebration)

O' Muhammad... we gave you a piece of heaven
She's your daughter... and they said you had no children
Be proud of her... she'll give you eleven princes
Take care of her... she'll sing for you heaven's praises
You're an orphan... but she'll treat you like you're her son

* * *

Bathed in divine light... she has descended
You recall heaven... when you ascended
From this child's neck, smell heaven's scent
Now heaven's with you in each moment

With your patience... for a child you awaited
From heaven's dust... your daughter we have created

* * *

They thought, childless... you were to grow old
So from heaven's throne... we have borrowed gold
Born and she smiles at your delight
Clenched your finger, the lady of light

You smile... and in awe, your eyes, she watches
She makes you laugh... and Zahra, your laugh, entrances

* * *

Remember heaven... a garden you walked
You saw there, a rose... with this rose you talked
From this garden this rose we lifted
Heaven's rose to your hands we gifted

You hold her... at your fingertips she chuckles
At Our mercy... Fatima Zahra, she smiles

You grew an orphan... your youth, motherless
Yet now you hold her... her forehead you kiss

No, none to soothe you is worthier
You hold the mother of her father

You'll raise her… so that Muhammad she can raise
You'll praise her… so, Ahmed, she'll defend and praise

* * *

Know that this present… with her shall not end
Eleven princes… through her we shall send
Each prince within your footsteps shall tread
Muhammad, they'll all be Muhammad

And every prince… will have the pride of their mother
Knowing that she… is a piece of the hereafter

* * *

(London – 03/05/13)

How Many Women Fall?
(In Lamentation)

Don't think only Fatima by the door was taken
Hajar and Maryam and Hawa found their ribs broken
How many women fall... between the door and wall?

* * *

From the house of Fatima they heard a roar
It was as if gold fell and shattered the floor
They ask the house and when they ask its tears pour
"How many women between the wall and door?

What fell, even thunder was embarrassed from its sound
What is worth so much that when it fell it hurt the ground?
What made the Earth's turn stall... between the door and wall?"

* * *

The greatest women from the holy Quran
Cried out in pain and found their ribs were broken
In tears, holding their ribs, they asked a question
"What happened to the leader of all women?

What fell and what broke, this pain is so unbearable
Were it placed on a mountain we would watch it crumble
Hearts to our mother crawl... between the door and wall"

* * *

I saw Hajar running, looking for water
Suddenly she forget the thirst within her
She felt the pain of the rib of Fatima
As if she's crushed between Safa and Marwa

She heard the voice of her mother Fatima was hushed
Between two mountains, the mountain of patience was crushed
From her mother she'd call... between the door and wall

* * *

I saw Maryam still pregnant with her son
Hearing the silence of her child within
She cries out as her mother's worries begin
"O' Fatima what happened to your Mohsin?

I swear, if you find that your son shall no longer live
Don't cry O' Fatima, my Eisa to you I'll give"
Child, mother and all… between the door and wall

* * *

I saw Hawa with Adam, and they wail
"What happened to the mother of the veil?"
"I know when I felt in my chest a nail
On her tears the ship of salvation set sail

Tell me why the light, from which I took all my shyness
Leaves this world in pain, in wailing and in her distress?
And her killer stands tall… between the door and wall"

* * *

I hear the voices of all women are hushed
When into the house of Fatima they rushed
It wasn't just Fatima by the door crushed
It wasn't just her veil by fire brushed

Every lover of our lady Fatima Zahra
Screams out in their pain hearing of the door and fire
Nothing broken was small… between the door and wall

* * *

(London – 30/01/14)

Forgive Me
(In Lamentation)

Forgive me if I shed tears

* * *

Forgive me if when these days return to us… you see that tear-drops on my eyelid lie
But you can't understand what my eyes see… each time they see her, I feel my heart die
I see her crushed between the door and wall… each time my eyelids close and crush my eye
And as blood flows from the chest of Zahra… my tears flow to soothe the pain of my eye

* * *

Forgive me if when day reaches the sky… and I see her days on the horizon
I hold onto my chest in agony… as if the rib in my chest is broken
As if I'm crushed between a door and wall… gasping for air as the door would tighten
With the pain of a nail in my chest… holding my scream because I'm a woman

* * *

Forgive me if I act like an orphan… crying out for the help of her father
Holding my scarf like I'm holding my soul… so it doesn't get burned by the fire
I sit with my hands defending my face… wondering if this man has a daughter
As the devil's hand slaps the purest face… and chains are put on the hands of Haider

* * *

Forgive me if when I see black cloth… my hand holds my heart, feeling a darkness

As if there is a gap deep in my heart... as if I have lost something so precious
As if I'm a mother who lost her son... and you see me holding him in sadness
Looking at someone too young to be born... too young to see his mother in distress

* * *

If these days I dress in black, forgive me... if I cry when I serve, recite or cook
If I'm serving and I collapse in tears... as if my soul the angel of death took
If the picture of Fatima Zahra... you see in my eyes whenever you look
But the fire of her house burnt my face... and by the push of the door I was shook

* * *

(Los Angeles - 16/01/14)

If You Had Known
(In Lamentation)

Today I see roses wither... all that is water turns to stone
All that was loved and comforted... is left uncared for and alone
A woman cries and breaks my heart... the pain in her voice shatters bone
She sits beside her father's grave... crying, father, if you had known

This is Fatima... with no-one beside her...
The grave of her father... it gives her no answer
Her wounds are torture... all she can remember...
Are nails and fire... and crying for Haider

* * *

Against the darkness of the night... alone to his grave, she'd complain
The roses beside him are drowned... her tears upon these roses rain
A daughter yearns her father's hand... to soothe the wounds that bring her pain
But even if these wounds heal... her memories, they still remain

Daily she'd recall... the door against the wall...
As Ali she would call... pierces her the nail
The moon, stars and all... falls with her if she'd fall...
Upon a broken rib... alone, she would wail

* * *

Father you left me in a flame... everything burns in your absence
Now all my eyes see is fire... and it calls out for your presence
O' my father from the fire... turns to ashes, all my patience
I came covered in these ashes... but all I heard was your silence

To where do I turn... if my father I yearn...
No-one came to heal... the burns on this orphan
In fire I burn... cry for me, my children...
My heart's turned to ashes... wanting you to return

* * *

NOURI SARDAR

To you I was like a mother... a mother's child is her heart
His presence brings to her heart joy... and her heart breaks when they're apart
Even if I could bear the pain... I felt the pain of Mohsin start
And from the light of daughter... I felt torn from my light, a part

This light was Mohsin... the last of my children...
The first to be taken... my heart would be broken
The door would open... my chest would be beaten...
Till from your beloved... my child had fallen

* * *

(London – 17/02/14)

Marriage of Ali and Fatima

(In Celebration)

Heaven and Earth celebrate… a marriage that's meant to be
No-one could marry Zahra… if there was never Ali

* * *

Descends from the Heavens, roses… and around their feet they scatter
She who is made from Heaven's dust… for the one born in the Ka'ba
On her wedding she taught us all… when that beggar had approached her
You can only have an Ali… if you are a Fatima

The Ka'ba and the Heavens… both give their children away
No-one could marry Zahra… if there was never Ali

* * *

A man born in the house of God… a woman made from paradise
In her eyes he saw only care… in his eyes she saw sacrifice
Like Ali lifted Khaybar's door… she lifted off his shoulders, vice
In return he gave her his soul… hoping that this soul would suffice

The eyes windows to the soul… in her eyes, his soul he'd see
No-one could marry Zahra… if there was never Ali

* * *

They are perfect for each-other… because only God each eye sees
Two lights became one forever… just like the greeting of two seas
I'll tell you why their household has… the greatest of family trees
As the leader of all women… had the simplest of all dowries

When men would ask Mohammed… he'd reply, "it's destiny
No-one could marry Zahra… if there was never Ali"

* * *

Ask yourselves, when Ali proposed… would Mohammed have turned his face
If he wasn't Bani Hashim… or was of a different race
Look how simple it was for him… shyness to his face you could trace
Yet when Ahmed heard he loved her… he pulled Ali towards his embrace

He takes Ali by his hand… and asks him, "Are you ready?
No-one could marry Zahra… if there was never Ali"

* * *

Look how beautiful it all is… she accepts him with her silence
And when they steal what is his… her voice is of loud defiance
The meeting of Earth and Heaven… an infinite, divine balance
As Ali, the father of dust… married Heaven's fragrance

The meeting of divine worlds… cries the Lord that made this day:
No-one could marry Zahra… if there was never Ali

* * *

All men have had their wife's name… at birth, written on their foreheads
But today Shia see written… 'Ali' and 'Zahra' on their heads
There won't be another Ali… and a Fatima no man weds
But in the service of these lights… each Shia newlywed treads

In every Shia wedding… cries both the mind and body:
No-one could marry Zahra… if there was never Ali

* * *

(London – 04/02/14)

THE UNDYING FLAME

Poetry in memory of the Master of Martyrs (pbuh)

"Yes, a thousand years have passed
Ten thousand years it'll last
For it lives in our memory
As if of yesterday's past"

Opening Verses III (Muharram)

Ashura's a School

Ashura's a school of lessons… Hussain taught me defiance
Abbas taught me selflessness… Zainab, she taught me patience
Qassim taught me sacrifice… death over life his preference
Layla gave Ali Akbar… Mohammed's last resemblance
Between the hands of Hussain… Hurr taught me repentance
Aabis taught me insanity… is but a lover's science
Ashura was not a day… its timelessness its brilliance
It repeats daily in the heart… always a beacon of guidance

The Call

For one lady, this night we recall
When descends the moon upon nightfall
It kneels on its skies, clouds to it crawl
The day that set Umaya's downfall
("Haya 'ala salah")
Come to prayer? No, not this call at all
("Haya 'alal falah")
Come to success? Success he'd enthrall
("Haya 'ala khayr il'amal")
The best of deeds? Deeds upon him fall
Ummul Baneen, today you recall
When "haya 'alal Abbas" was Fatima's call
You cry in pride with Yazid's downfall
Blessing Mohammed, Ali and all

If It Was Never for Hussain

Hussain and if it was never for Hussain
You'd see their mother's names children would forget

Hussain and if it was never for Hussain
You'd see babies when they're fed remain upset

Hussain and if it was never for Hussain
You'd see sunrise starting a war with sunset

Hussain and if it was never for Hussain
You would see the moon demanding the earth's debt

Hussain and if it was never for Hussain
Moons would complain that their suns don't ever set

Hussain and if it was never for Hussain
Letting us breathe air the same air would regret,

Hussain and if it was never for Hussain
There'd be no H, S or N in alphabet

Hussain and if it was never for Hussain
The word 'freedom' in dictionaries none would let

Hussain and if it was never for Hussain
You'd see hearts of stone and no cheek with tears wet

Hussain and if it was never for Hussain
Oppressors would oppress without fear of threat

If suffices to say were there no Hussain
On the day of Ashura none would have wept

And none to recite blessings on Mohammed
When with their ears the name of Mohammed met

The Banner

Find me alone and sad and heartbroken
Find me with grey hairs as away I wither
Find me happy with a smile on my face
Find me content, young and full of honour
Find me at the edge of this Earth, in silence
Find me living next door, a cheerful neighbour
Wherever you find me, I'll be at the same place:
Tying rope on the standard of Hussain's banner

* * *

Your Day

(In lamentation)

It was not just a day witnessed... by your eyes, by your eyes
Millions witness your day so... hear their cries, hear their cries
Hussain, you are not alone... your pain to millions is shown
Millions witness your day so... hear their cries, hear their cries

* * *

Between your eyelid and eye... drawn in every tear you'd cry
You'd stand alone, asking for help... and did you ever ask why?

Calamities you witnessed... left our own eyes so distressed
That we'd cry as if horses' hooves... were on our own fathers pressed

You stood alone on that day... every love taken away
When alone you spoke to your Lord... behind you we'd come and pray

Yes, a thousand years have passed... ten thousand years it'll last
For it lives in our memory... as if of yesterday's past

They spoke of you as if you died... and your plight, and your plight
Instead you brought our souls to life... with your light, with your light
Your pain is not yours to own... your pain to millions is shown
Millions witness your day so... hear their cries, hear their cries

* * *

Alone, when for help you called... your loneliness we recalled
Yet your voice, it transcended time... and by it we were enthralled
A broken heart none could mend... to wind your hand you'd extend
Expecting someone to help you... brings you a silence, this wind
We watched you stand there alone... and cried out, to you we'll come
Yet you turned away in sadness... hearing no voice and no-one
It gave us such a heartache... that when we mourn, the worlds shake
And whilst you sleep in your sadness... our grief still keeps us awake
We came running when we heard help... you needed, you needed
We begged our Lord to reach your side... and pleaded, and pleaded
For our lateness we'd atone... your pain to millions is shown
Millions witness your day so... hear their cries, hear their cries

* * *

With the rise of your day's dawn... pictures on your eye were drawn
And when we asked for but a glimpse... uncontrollably we'd mourn
We saw a young, orphaned prince... asking your permission, since
You were the one father he had... his death challenged your patience
In your arms you held your son... and you complained to the sun
Can I not bring Ali water... not a drop rests on my tongue
We saw later, in your arms... fingers clenched by tiny palms
The infant's neck, that you once kissed... a three-headed arrow harms
When we saw what your eyes saw we... wouldn't sleep, wouldn't sleep
When we would gaze at our children... we would weep, we would weep
His blood to the sky you'd thrown... your pain to millions is shown
Millions witness your day so... hear their cries, hear their cries

* * *

Asking to feel what you felt... by your remains we all knelt
Soothing your wounds with our own hands... our tears, the sun's heat would melt

We felt on your back a weight... preyed on your innocence, hate
Not what you are, for who you are... you embraced a headless fate

From your eyes, waterless tears... every time reaches your ears
The cries of these sonless mothers... you'd cry out, "take me O' spears!"

Every loved one was taken... you'd cry, he'd not awaken
"With your death O' my flagbearer... now my back has been broken"

With remnants of your ink, sorrow... you would draw, you would draw
We'd follow its trail, your pain... we all saw, we all saw
You stood ageless, as we'd grown... your pain to millions is shown
Millions witness your day so... hear their cries, hear their cries

* * *

On that day, alone you stood... the trials that you withstood
Carved lessons into history... that we read and understood

You stood up to a tyrant... and withstood every moment
Of your torture, of your slaughter... and we saw your achievement

BEGINNING & END

You rose up and so we rose… oppression we would oppose
And before humiliation… death we demanded and chose

We told all that death had lied… because Hussain never died
He lives on, he is immortal… for our tears, his death defied

On your day, millions of eyes… on you gaze, on you gaze
They cry hearing of your tale… and your ways, and you ways
I wonder if, then, you'd known… your pain to millions is shown
Millions witness your day so… hear their cries, hear their cries

* * *

(Najaf – 27/11/12)

Hussain's Worth

Seven letters of which, daily, I've dreamt
And to each letter, a lifetime I have lent
His name touches my ears before my heart's consent
The beat of my heart skips, a lover's moment
The joy of my smile and the cries I lament
Yet I still wonder what "Hussain" truly meant

* * *

My eyes see bodies on desert's plains, they lied
Yet their names lived on, though upon dust they lied
Whoever said Hussain is dead, they lied
He lives in the heart of every believer

* * *

He preached revolution, alone with his sole sword
He defeated swords with blood and with his sole sword
Hussain didn't die that day, rather his soul soared
His name is a symbol that flies forever

* * *

The worth of Hussain is none know of his worth
His story the greatest story ever told
And even though daily we hear his name
The sheer value of his worth remains untold
Hussain bent the meaning of the word 'impossible'
Just like his grave bends the scale of this world
His name redefines what is most valuable
Like his dust is sought more than diamond and gold

* * *

He cannot be killed, no matter how much they try
The perfect imbalance against all who oppress
Over one-thousand years, his enemies gone
In every age they fail, whilst he sees success
I tell you Hussain defies infinity
He has the only love that's timeless
21 million walking is my proof
Let 6 billion walk, he isn't worth less

* * *

Hussain bends the scale of mortality
His existence alters the meaning of 'real'
And he who gets to know Aba Abdillah
Finds nothing surprising, nothing surreal
Medicine in this world, saviour in the next
Not just illnesses, hearts and souls he'd heal
If mankind knew what he was capable of
You'd see kings of nations at his grave kneel

* * *

I tell you that there is only one Hussain
Till time's end there can never be a second
Bring me any noble fighter of justice
On a scale, Hussain equals a thousand
He's great without pride, this adds to his greatness
In his lovers' pride his greatness is mentioned
He lived simply, we gave him a shrine of gold
As poets say, he deserves one of diamond

* * *

If you're told he died that know that they lied
Open your eyes and give your pupils consent
He's the symbol of freedom for all oppressed
Hussain in every uprising is present
And it is not just his shrine that holds his flag
In each of our hearts he has a monument
I tell you his worth is that he never died
He is loved and adored in every moment

* * *

A sun and glorious in your rise
Revolution O' Hussain in your rise
A sun in my eyes and in your eyes
You see daily to your rise I surrender

* * *

(London – 16/06/13)

Silent I Leave

(In lamentation)

Goodbyes they've said... are best unsaid
Silent I leave O' Mohammed

* * *

They say speak words to who you love... and bid farewell in your silence
So at your grave, silent I stand... left torn apart by your absence
For your Badr and your Uhud... they seek my blood for their vengeance
I see my death before my eyes... and with it smell Heaven's fragrance

Not what I am... for who I am
To battle your beloved is led
Silent I leave O' Mohammed

* * *

I stand withered beside your grave... and scatter upon it roses
These roses beside you shall grow... whilst your beloved, death approaches
O' grandfather, when they blossom... your beloved Karbala reaches
And the day they wither away... your beloved's head a spear raises

As each rose grows... grows your sorrows
Till to death's hand Hussain is fed
Silent I leave O' Mohammed

* * *

They say to gift but a present... toward your love before you leave
And to you my life I present... so that in my absence you grieve
And your absence O' grandfather... shows me how love, it can deceive
I gift to you what I have left... so your happiness I achieve

That which you want... shall my soul haunt
Yet I welcome my death and dread

NOURI SARDAR

Silent I leave O' Mohammed

* * *

I cannot speak from my heartache… so I let you see and listen
You see alone in a far land… your Hussain and what will happen
You see on us, the pangs of thirst… a camp full of thirsty women
A camp that when I die shall burn… taking captive every orphan

This our future… for it prepare
For they'll complain to you, Ahmed
Silent I leave O' Mohammed

* * *

Despite my tears, O' grandfather… I want you to my courage heed
I will not let a tyrant rule… a revolution I shall lead
It matters not if my body… upon Karbala's dust shall bleed
And if my Lord wants my head raised… upon a spear, than I am pleased

I shall revolt… for I was taught
To be free and never oppressed
Silent I leave O' Mohammed

* * *

It matters not, if from my thirst… nations shall weep and remember
Or if taken from my body… is my head and raised on a spear
It matters not if my child… within my arms they would murder
I'll throw his blood toward the sky… and complain to my Creator

When blood shall rain… know that Hussain
Has been killed and severed, his head
Silent I leave O' Mohammed

* * *

(Istanbul – 13/11/12)

Jibraeel's Wings

(In lamentation)

As Shimr's sword for the blood of Ali sings
Every eye turns to look at Jibraeel's wings
Protect him, protect him... with your two wings, protect him

* * *

When the dust of war settled... and every man had battled... for Hussain
Every body lies there torn... over their sons, mothers mourn... none remain
Only remains, Shimr's sword... so thirsty for divine blood... so insane
All watch as its blade, it rests... upon the holiest neck... they complain

O' you who wished to be the sixth of the five
Fold up your two wings and toward the Earth dive
Rescue him, rescue him... with your two wings, protect him
Protect him, protect him... with your two wings, protect him

* * *

The Prophets, they watch in shock... as Shimr and his sword mock... Mohammed
In anguish toward their Lord... for his protection they called... tears they shed
Holding their tears in their palms... to wiping Jibraeel's arms... they were led
O' Jibraeel, they all cried... how often have your wings dried... blood he's bled

He found himself by the Prophets surrounded
As the chest of Hussain, Shimr's sword pounded
Defend him, defend him... with your two wings, protect him
Protect him, protect him... with your two wings, protect him

* * *

A sight that no-one can bear... it makes angels wish to tear... off their eyes
Every angel turns away... to Jibraeel gazes sway... there he lies
You stand, a mighty mountain... when collapsed has this Hussain... and he cries
Your wings, from your Lord, a gift... in your wings his body lift... to the skies

O' mountain raise the body that is frail
Upon Mohammed horses wish to trample
Embrace him, embrace him... with your two wings, protect him
Protect him, protect him... with your two wings, protect him

* * *

Arrives, the angel of death... from all his grief, out of breath... and he speaks
O' Jibraeel it is time... as the seconds in this crime... become weeks
Imprisons me, my duty... the tears I weep are mighty... on my cheeks
Will you embrace your power... every soul for your answer... waits and seeks

The weight of my duty crushes my shoulders
Approaches our beloved, Yazid's soldiers
Fight for him, fight for him... with your two wings, protect him
Protect him, protect him... with your two wings, protect him

* * *

In the place of hands that fell... grew the wings of an angel... and he comes
The lion of might and zeal... a child, from what he feels... he becomes
Jibraeel, I am the moon... I can't protect, from my tomb... Ali's sons
I have wings, but they don't let... Abbas, his master protect... and death hums

I hear death singing the name of my Master
Do what I cannot and defend my brother
Run to him, run to him... with your two wings, protect him
Protect him, protect him... with your two wings, protect him

BEGINNING & END

* * *

Then Jibraeel hears a voice… I'm Zainab, you have no choice… protect him
I'm the mother of sorrow… the pains of my tomorrow… sing a hymn
I know, if he cuts his head… centuries of hurt and dread… it's bring
In one wing his head you'll hold… and his body you will fold… in one wing

To the Heavens with this sight you shall return
And your wings the pangs of his anguish will burn
Surround him, surround him… with your two wings, protect him
Protect him, protect him… with your two wings, protect him

* * *

He folds his wings and he dives… armoured against swords and knives… he's plated
He plunges toward the Earth… Shimr upon Ali's worth… is weighted
He cuts his neck, vein to vein… by the devil's sword, Hussain… is greeted
Jibraeel's wings arrive late… and Hussain's head, Yazid's plate… awaited

With his two wings Jibraeel strikes his head
And sees Zainab mourning like him just ahead
Forgive me, forgive me… tell your brother, forgive me
Forgive me, forgive me… tell your brother, forgive me

* * *

(Karbala – 09/11/12)

A Heartbreaking Goodbye
(In lamentation)

I hear this farewell every single year… when Hussain's day is near
A heart-breaking goodbye is all I hear

* * *

After every loved one to death has fallen… Hussain comes to her tent
He sees through her two eyes, her heart is broken… and his daughters lament
He kisses her head, Fatima's last orphan… to grief, her heart he's sent

She holds his shirt and cries… loneliness in her eyes
For one last time, his eyes into hers' peer
A heart-breaking goodbye is all I hear

* * *

She clenches his hand, not wanting him to leave… Hussain is all she knew
Your death is one thing to see, but to believe… my beloved ones are few
Your absence alone till my death I would grieve… and together we grew

With me since I was young… "goodbye" upon my tongue
If I let you go, would you reappear?
A heart-breaking goodbye is all I hear

* * *

She holds him close, smelling his scent one last time… drenching his shirt with tears
The comfort and love I gave your heart from mine… you leave for swords and spears
The sun sets in my eyes, tell me what for what crime… and the night on me peers

I live your final day… it takes Hussain away
I bid goodbye to what I held most dear

A heart-breaking goodbye is all I hear

* * *

O' brother, let my hands adjust your armour… with death you'll look handsome
Don't let blood pour from the wounds of Zahra's rose… with death, a rose become
Take care of your skin as you're mother you'll face… when death to you shall come

Of this moment they've dreamt… go and live this moment
To wash your blood I've left tear upon tear
A heart-breaking goodbye is all I hear

* * *

His children, some are too young to understand… he leaves them all with her
He walks and they run and grab onto his hand… he looks at each daughter
O' my daughters go and beside your aunt stand… let go of your father

He let go of each one… beside him is no-one
The lion of God departs without fear
A heart-breaking goodbye is all I hear

* * *

He walks and in tears Zainab cries out his name… you're the son of Ali
How many times I've cried and running you came… don't leave me, don't leave me
You're all I knew when orphans we both became… look at this tragedy

Me, you'd never displease… let me die with you, please
Even in death let me to you be near
A heart-breaking goodbye is all I hear

* * *

(London – 09/06/13)

The Killing - Al Maqtal

(In lamentation)

I beg you Shimr, don't sever his head
Bring your sword to me and take mine instead

He sits on his chest, and watches Zainab run
Beside her brother no brothers & no-one
"Is there any to help me?" No there is none
In her hopelessness to her brother she fled

She screams to Shimr," leave my brother alone
The arrows cutting him for his pain atone
The cuts on his body have reached his bone
And the dust weeps for holding the blood he's bled"

"Leave him alone, maybe he'll reawaken
You sit on his chest whilst his back is broken"
His eyes watch Zainab by her grief stricken
He watches her as he severs Hussain's head

She sits by him massacred by his absence
His body is here but where is his presence?
Everything is broken, except his silence
And nothing was left of him unless it bled

She screams as if her soul from her body leaps
"My brother in a river of his blood sleeps"
She slaps her head so hard that for her he weeps
As his severed head towards a spear is led

"O' head I once adored in awe of its height
O' head that once embarrassed the moon's night
O' head, not only are your girls left in fright
They see your head placed on a spear, drenched blood-red
As if massacring you wasn't enough
And neither was tearing these girls' hearts in half
We watch the spear that holds your holy head laugh
So today's grief would match yesterday's bloodshed

My eye scarred by seeing your head on a spear
The tears I cry are blood, tortures me each tear
I see the lion that other lions fear
With a severed neck into a spear embed

If you don't care for him, care for his children
At least let this head from their eyes be hidden
You torment the little hearts of each orphan
Telling them, to Shimr's sword, Hussain was fed"

They killed her brother and left him with no shroud
They raise his head, and raise it as if they're proud
Taking his women captive before a crowd
And curse his father as to Yazid they head

"O' grandfather two of him were torn apart
O' grandfather his head from body they'd part
O' grandfather nothing would have soothed his heart
Except your kiss upon his holy forehead

O' grandfather, killed with no-one beside him
He looked to the distance, and saw only them
The silence of the wind sang a painful hymn
Telling him you're alone and alone you tread

If my father knows just how we are treated
How is a spear with my brother's head weighted
Indeed the sword my brother's blood defeated
But we're left to fight this sword's vengeance and dread

O' lion of battle, to which battle crawls
O' catcher of the flag if, ever, it falls
We're left paraded in Yazid's courts and halls
Through torture, death & pain, these women I've lead"

After they steal his head as they wail
They take her captive and his Zainab they steal
Leaving, in her, a wound only he could heal
After they killed him, her brother they'd behead

(London – 02/10/13)

Crying in My Sleep
(In lamentation)

I hear your voice when I sleep… telling me to for you weep
How much in love I've become… I close my eyes and you come…
Telling me to for you weep

* * *

Much like a man that is crazed… or one that is left amazed…
When I drift off to sleep, I hear
I hear the voice of someone… left in a land, all alone…
And trickles from my eye, a tear
The coldness of this tear-drop… makes me, from my sleep, wake up…
I hear screaming from ear to ear
O' sleeper can you forget… even for but a moment…
What happened to my household here?
Can you forget all I've seen… or how much in love you've been…
A love that you say you can't bear
If I'm hurt would you forget… I'm hurt when your tears are wet…
I watch upon you everywhere

I wake up crying his name… my forgetfulness, a shame
I see where this voice comes from… I close my eyes and you come
Telling me to for you weep

* * *

O' lover, how can you sleep… when from my wounds, my tears seep
When no-one laments my absence
How can your two eyes stay closed… when to me death is proposed…
Circled by swords is Heaven's prince
I've seen nothing but closed eyes… a demise after demise…
My women, they have not slept since
If you're truly my lover… would off to sleep you wonder…
When I'm in need of assistance?
I walk this desert alone… my enemies won't atone…
Pounded by swords is my patience
And to my death I wander… calling out for a helper…
You wander off to a distance

How can you embrace your dreams... from my eyes a river streams
You cry and you're so alone... I close my eyes and you come
Telling me to for you weep

* * *

Would I choose to hear this voice... do I even have a choice...
When he gave, for me, everything
And can I ever let go... I hear his name and tears flow...
He's become a part of my being
Much like a man that's in love... I gaze at the skies above...
And only his name I'm seeing
And when I look at the ground... his severed body I've found...
And I soothe it with my weeping
I hold my dreams in one hand... yet they flutter in his wind...
When to my heart Hussain's speaking
In the other, I see him... he sings me a painful hymn...
And I am left helpless watching

I am torn between two worlds... worlds apart and this household
For Hussain what have I done... I close my eyes and you come
Telling me to for you weep

* * *

You sleep and wander your dreams... how real your dreams can seem...
Alone I wander this desert
Approaches you, all your hopes... as I walk upon death's slopes...
And too few eyes for me are wet
Your hopes approach, a fountain... death comes to me, a mountain...
To bear its weight alone, my test
You taste its water's sweetness... I embrace such a harshness...
A mountain that crushes my chest
Would from your sweet dreams you drink.. when from such a weight, I sink..
Upon my shoulders its weight rests
And for assistance I call... and toward my grave I fall...
Shimr's sword upon my neck rests

Your hopes and your dreams you face... a sword I'm forced to embrace
Something that can't be undone... I close my eyes and you come
Telling me to for you weep

BEGINNING & END

* * *

I wake up and sit in shame… and on my mind plays his name…
Just like the love of the lover
I raise my head, I see drawn… before me a fallen crown…
The crown of his father, Haider
If by my dreams I'm taunted… by the swords he is hunted…
in his battle, a lone soldier
I grab my heart as a shield… and head to his battlefield…
With my love for him, my armour
My dreams become his desert… I see what he can't forget…
As I step onto Karbala
I hear the voices of men… Habib tells me with his pen…
Get up and assist your Master

I complain to him in tears… between us, a thousand years
And with my regret, I hum… I close my eyes and you come
Telling me to for you weep

* * *

O' child, you want to serve… let your gaze toward me swerve…
Let this picture rest in your mind
Watch me holding my child… expecting water, mild…
An arrow in his neck I find
Watch me telling each mother… that death is their son's future…
And to martyrdom they're inclined
I feel nothing but death… and I yearn for my last breath…
My hardships in my blood I've signed
If truly you're part of me… you'd feel my tragedy…
For lovers pains are intertwined
Hasten to me in mourning… it's your name I am calling…
My lovers are my pain defined

I see nothing but beauty… when you wake and weep for me
And we become a soul, one… I close my eyes and you come
Telling me to for you weep

* * *

(London – 22/01/13)

A Promise
(In lamentation)

A promise to you I'll give… it repeats in every breath
Every breath of mine tells you… I'll mourn you until my death

* * *

I swear and by the Earth's turn… the sunrise and the sunset
By the growth and death of life… by every dead soul's regret
I can forget everything… Hussain I'll never forget

Valueless all else became
To me, nothing is the same
I'll die repeating your name

All else is forgettable… whilst your name sweetens my breath

* * *

Your love to me, more than love… a medicine to each pain
My mother's duty to you… that through her, you, I'd attain
She'd write upon my cradle… "This, a servant of Hussain"

This forever my purpose
My comfort in my distress
To serve Hussain and Abbas

A servant I'll always remain… both in life and after death

* * *

My lullabies were about you… as all else would make me wail
Every child felt protected… by angels who rocked their cradle
But from my cradle to my grave… I saw, by me, Abu Fadhil
I grew up watching his height
Whilst comforted by his might
The only moon in my night

And whenever I heard his name… I was left dazed, without breath

* * *

Ensuring that none reside there… I saw at the gate of my heart
I'd let none in, but when you came… I'd run to tear this gate apart
In my heart I'd build you a shrine… asking you, don't ever depart

I don't know love from hatred
But this love I've awaited
And for it was created

It was purpose within life… and remained long after my death

* * *

All that was in me was worthless… but with you, it became priceless
Why worry about what is lost… when Hussain's blessings are endless
If they put the world in my hand… I wouldn't trade it for your service

Give me no silver and no gold
No beloved and no household
And you as priceless I'll still hold

As long as I breath O' Hussain… I gift toward you every breath

* * *

Though on me fell the whole world's weight… with two names I found nothing hard
Compare me to shattered glass… with pride upon every shard
Abu Fadhil holds my back… holds my hand, Abu Sajjad

If I fall and my eye cries
Abbas pushes me to rise
And my tears Hussain's hand dries

They remind me of my purpose… to serve them until my death

* * *

(London – 31/10/13)

Hussain Never Died
(In lamentation)

In the tears that we've cried… "Hussain had never died"
An immortal revolution… Hussain, Hussain

* * *

Just as the seven skies with the horizon are bound
We are bound to Hussain and with him our heads we crowned
If the skies fall toward earth then catches it, the ground
And in the beauty of the skies, Hussain's name we found

We caught him when he fell… and there was no farewell
Not by death, by our hearts taken… Hussain, Hussain

* * *

Artists draw beauty with beauty and beauty appears
When I draw the name of Hussain, I draw it with tears
And yet this beauty can create the greatest of fears
When a tyrant upon the legend of Hussain peers

In his calamity… Hussain blossomed beauty
A rose that leaves tyrants shaken… Hussain, Hussain

* * *

Hussain conquers hearts, infact he conquers everything
The Heavens saw Hussain and it made Hussain its king
On a scale, nothing's like him, bring me anything
Bring me a mountain of gold and Hussain I will bring

No-one knows of his worth… his murder shook the Earth
For him the Lord's throne would open… Hussain, Hussain

* * *

No-one reached immortality, but to him it bends

And Heaven must be earned but for Hussain it descends
All that rises falls, but Hussain forever ascends
Every story ends but Hussain's tale never ends

He changed all that we know… testifies tears that flow
The sun to which we'd awaken… Hussain, Hussain

* * *

They said there's a flame in our hearts, no, it's not just a flame
A fire that engulfs all oppression it became
Hussain's love is a pride and proudly with it we came
And burned tyrants to ashes with love that brought them shame

When Hussain's flag flutters… all tyranny flutters
Evil falls when his name's spoken… Hussain, Hussain

* * *

Hussain bends the scale of what's possible and fair
Only Hussain can be killed and yet bring them despair
When they die they don't just die, Hussain burns out their air
The veins of tyrants from their necks Hussain's hand would tear

Every tyrant fears him… his murder challenged them
In his eyes their end is written… Hussain, Hussain

* * *

Hussain's immortal as the tears we cry testify
Revolutions are born with each teardrop that we cry
And if any demand we stop, what do we reply
He taught us, no humiliation, we'd rather die

Revolution he taught… to us freedom he brought
And we want the world to listen… Hussain, Hussain

* * *

We cry out a scream of pride and none could be prouder
"Hussain's our leader, what a blessing of a leader"
He never died, they lied, he is something of wonder
Every uprising is led by the son of Haider

BEGINNING & END

Hussain is immortal… and he'll never fail,
Immortal, his inspiration… Hussain, Hussain

* * *

(Beirut - 13/12/13)

Every Moment
(In lamentation)

Every moment... for your servant... is like a dream
It's an honour... for you Master... that our tears stream

* * *

From the cradle, by my mother... your love I was given and taught
She fed me the milk of your name... and you became my every thought
And in my cradle I would cry... by your tragedy left distraught
When I was young... like this I'd mourn... until my hands to hit I'd taught

And so I grew... in loving you... and knowing you
My years would pass... Knowing Abbas... and knowing you

* * *

At a young age, I saw a dream... where men would read on your pulpit
I stood in awe, as they would draw... your day with words of a poet
They drew your thirst, and your heartache... when tents would burn, your daughters hit
I saw this day... as clear as day... every year this day I'd visit

And when I woke... from dreams, I spoke... and cried your name
I would lament... as your servant... And cried your name

* * *

As I grew up, your love it grew... we were like one, a soul and heart
And I served you, because I knew... I'd see you when from life I'd part
And yearly when for you I'd mourn... my soul it would be torn apart
I gave my youth... my days to you... from my heart you'd never depart

Every trial... Was all while... You were watching
If I'd smile... If I'd wail... You were watching

* * *

When I had children I'd recall... my mother and how she raised me

I told my sons when they were born... I gift you to his tragedy
And to my daughters I'd tell them... of Zainab, daughter of Ali
My whole household... to you I sold... so they'd serve you long after me
When I married... For you I grieved... We were for you
My wife I taught... Hussain she sought... We were for you

* * *

When I died and I was buried... I cried your name, wanted your sight
If I served you for all my years... I thought you'd save me with my plight
And in my grave I was questioned... I saw coming to me a light
I saw Hussain... I cried his name... on Heaven's door, my name he'd write
My friends mourned me... With my family... And I smiled
They were in pain... I saw Hussain... And I smiled

* * *

(London – 13/11/12)

With Your Love

(In lamentation)

With everything, patient... with your love, impatient
Daily, you, I lament... Hussain

* * *

He whose name sleeps in my heart... and there, it tears it apart
My eyes, windows to the beauty of your name
Seven letters that I've loved... form to become my beloved
With my heartbeat, part of my blood you became

I searched for your beauty... and found it within me
In me, a tragedy... Hussain

* * *

With or without intention... your love crowned my creation
And in smiles and cries, it became my pride
If in sadness, my tears pour... I sit, weeping, at your door
And till your hand comforts me, there I reside

My heart like an orphan's... at your touch it softens
And my love it becomes... Hussain

* * *

To a servant, a master... or to a son, a father
Your love became one of comfort and of care
Daily, I'd wake and recall... how, in the night, you I'd call
With the sunrise and sunset, your love I'd share

On one side a beloved... whilst I want to be loved
By one, never unloved... Hussain

* * *

If deep in my heart you sleep... you wake when for you I weep
And you see me torn apart for your trials
When rivers of tears I shed... you present to me your head

And its ears hear the sweetness of our wails
If for you I lament… you hear every moment
And to me you present… Hussain

* * *

Flowing deep within my blood… your name flows as a beloved
It feels everything I think and feel
Your love to my heart you taught… you became my every thought
At your greatness my destiny would kneel

Entranced by your greatness… root of my happiness
Ka'ba of my sadness… Hussain

* * *

I surrendered my sorrow… whilst you became my shadow
And it draws pictures of your trials and pain
All else, became meaningless… my life became your sadness
And in my heart's soil I planted Hussain

Your day I remembered… to it, I surrendered
By one, I was honoured… Hussain

* * *

(London – 13/04/13)

This Wound
(In lamentation)

You've left a wound in each lover

* * *

Amongst all of creation, you've captured our gaze
Even the swords, thirsty for your blood, sing you praise
The spear cries out, when your severed head, it would raise
Bathed in your blood, it knows your name none could erase

They see that you last forever… you've left a wound in each lover

* * *

On the plains of heavenly dust your blood was shed
It complains of the burden that, on it, you bled
Instead of rain, divine blood its soil was fed
And it makes weep whichever men upon it tread

Your blood scarred it, like a river… you've left a wound in each lover

* * *

We grew up in the shadow of your brilliance
We only know mere tales of your existence
Was it not enough that destroyed us, your absence?
The story of your killing destroyed our patience

On your torture we would ponder… you've left a wound in each lover

* * *

In every age, the sheer weight of your love is yearned
And only in the face of hardship is it earned
Every heart that felt orphaned toward you was turned
And in the flame of your love all our trials burned

To your comfort we would wander… you've left a wound in each lover

* * *

Would it be that in grief you wandered to the sword
Or that with death you felt comforted by your Lord?
Death called you, but from the cradle your name we've called
Only a soulless and headless body answered

You've left our eyes with this picture… you've left a wound in each lover

* * *

Yet you taught us to oppression you never bowed
And with your head raised on a spear, it rises, proud
In awe of your greatness, watches, an entranced crowd
Your uncovered body billions of tears shroud

This wound lasts till the hereafter… you've left a wound in each lover

* * *

(London – 15/04/13)

My Life is Two Names
(In lamentation)

My life is two names / Abbas & Hussain
My eyes carry / one destiny:
Abbas & Hussain

* * *

I learnt to give my life one rule, watching its years pass,
Beyond the fence where two names reside, let none trespass
Hussain's name sleeps in my right eye, a name none surpass,
Look in my left eye, you'll see guarding it is Abbas

Two names in my heart / never torn apart
Two names of which none need ask me:
Abbas & Hussain

* * *

Beside two names, my place in the world I understood,
If I could reshape the world to shape their names, I would
From one I learnt to fear nothing, if alone I stood…
From one I learnt to raise my head high against falsehood

One, to me, priceless / the other, selfless,
From neither would I ever sway,
Abbas & Hussain

* * *

Two names that glowed in my eyes before any I met,
I can forget the world, but two names I can't forget
Perfect yet different like the sunrise and the sunset
If ever one sets, it awaits the rise of the next

A sun and a moon / a night and a noon
No night or day, my eyes just see
Abbas and Hussain

NOURI SARDAR

* * *

I saw one like a sun against tyrants had risen
Whilst the other raised the flag of his revolution
They were like one, back against back, against oppression
And when one fell it meant the other's back was broken

Never torn apart / Two sides of my heart
And the two beats of my heart say
Abbas and Hussain

* * *

Hussain bends one side of my mind, Abbas the other
On one side lies the tents, the other lies the river
I hear one cry forgive me, I couldn't bring water
The other cries, I'll forgive you, just call me brother

Safa and Marwa / torn in Karbala
Two names that torment me daily
Abbas and Hussain

* * *

(London - 13/11/13)

A Thousand Years
(In lamentation)

This love won't die... the tears we cry...
Have made you live a thousand years
And with each tear... your name shall last...
Beyond tens of thousands of years

* * *

A flag that has your name we've raised... and it flutters with our mourning
Its edges pierce the moon at night... and make it cry till the morning
Upon your day, it turns blood red... as grief for you it's adorning
And by the time the sun rises... it hears the moon for you calling

Even at night, when we mourn you...
The sun upon your lovers peers
And with each tear... your name shall last...
Beyond tens of thousands of years

* * *

We were born to this world, entranced... by love within seven letters
The "H" was you, the "U" was us... the "S"-es spoke of our secrets
The "A", your father's path we chose... the "I", the eye that, on you, peers
The "N" cemented our belief... they thought you died, we cried "never"

In each letter... we lived a life...
Soothed only by rivers of tears
And with each tear... your name shall last...
Beyond tens of thousands of years

* * *

A sea of tears, in which we bathed... and from them we created gowns
Your love become immortal pride... and evil within our tears drowns
It became that we became you... we mirrored your smiles and frowns

The world watched as your hand, in pride… lover after lover it crowns

> We became kings in your service…
> And drowned in such a love, our fears
> And with each tear… your name shall last…
> Beyond tens of thousands of years

* * *

We gifted to your name, our lives… a gift and not a sacrifice
A love worth lives, destinies, fates…. upon it none could put a price
And though we gift toward you fates… we only hope it can suffice
You stood for our faith to surpass… centuries of hatred and vice

> We gifted to your name, our souls…
> And each soul, into two, it tears
> And with each tear… your name shall last…
> Beyond tens of thousands of years

* * *

We shrouded our fears in our tears… and to the world, we became one
We mourned you yearly as we wished… and before us could stand no-one
We struck our chests, we struck our heads… and walking to your grave we'd come
And drenched in the blood of our veins… lost deep in your love we'd become

> And in each eye, the soul's window…
> The beauty of your name it peers
> And with each tear… your name shall last…
> Beyond tens of thousands of years

* * *

Within the path of your mourning, we awoke
And the tears would stream, when the tongue, your name, spoke
Seven letters within which we abided
Made us stand us one, and never divided
We were torn between weeping at your beauty
And weeping hearing of your calamity
Upon the sands of your love, we built houses

BEGINNING & END

And dressed them in black when your day approaches

* * *

In the shrouds of your grief, we dressed our children
Presenting each to you as if an orphan
Our intentions could never once be clouded
When our dead within your letters we shrouded
When threatened with the fate of an explosion
We ran to it, seeing in it, creation
For like moths we were attracted to your name
But unlike them, were left unharmed by your flame

* * *

Living a life consistently in mourning
Your name our actions are only adorning
Your love like the blood that flows within each head
And it appears if our tears or blood we shed
For you, we could not in our patience confide
Leading to everything except suicide
Lost and only in your love can we be found
Like the millions who to your grave are bound

* * *

(London – 20/03/13)

I'm from Heaven
(In lamentation)

Husseini, Abbasi... Karbalaei

* * *

I'm from Heaven and from Heaven I remain
I'm from the only land where miracles rain
I'm from the land that has Abbas and Hussain
If you're from Heaven you're... Karbalaei

* * *

For teaching me Hussain, I love my father
For teaching me Zainab, I love my mother
They told me love Hussain and love no other
On my forehead written... Karbalaei

* * *

A servant, even if they call me a king
Beside Hussain and Abbas I have nothing
I have nothing and I gave them everything
An honour to be called... Karbalaei

* * *

I serve and I never ask from the people
To be serving Hussain's servants I'm grateful
If I want something, I beg Abu Fadhil
That's why I'm proud to be... Karbalaei

* * *

If ever from the pain of the world I cried
I'd remember why Karbala is my pride
I'd remember Abu Fadhil is my guide
Like Abu Fadhil I'm... Karbalaei

* * *

I am the son of Hussain and of Ali
All I have is Hussain and his tragedy
I'm Karbalaei because I'm Husseini
All I am, Hussaini… Karbalaei

* * *

(London – 07/06/13)

Our Beloved's Praise
(In lamentation)

O' Hussain all that which falls from the seeds of our sorrow
Shall grow into roses to be plucked by you tomorrow

Not a single beat of blood... escapes our beloved's gaze
And when for him love escapes... it sings our beloved's praise
For every tear and every wound that bleeds
Hussain extends his hand and intercedes

* * *

On a trail we walk... silence, there is no talk
Watching millions flock... to the beacon of love
Beneath each eye, a tear... on it, not age, no year
Upon it angels peer... from the Heavens above
Forgotten: life and things... the greatest dreams he brings
Every dream folds its wings... perched by him like a dove
Lost, only by him found... destinies to him bound
Existence, by him crowned... the greatest form of love

Every love placed beside his... faltered in embarrassment
If love lasted a whole age... his love transcended moment
Blossomed what was planted in us as seeds
Hussain extends his hand and intercedes

* * *

When a bird left his nest... it was never at rest
In striking its own chest... it would announce its pain
Master, we would gather... lamenting together
There was none worthier... of our grief, but Hussain
In heightened emotion... we challenged creation
Rise and fall may nation... but one name shall remain
As each man lamented... you'd find, illustrated
That with grief we've greeted... the Master of Youth, slain

Our hands knew of their purpose... to make men for you wither

In striking our chests we'd see… joining us, your own mother
She cries out to he who poetry reads
Hussain extends his hand and intercedes

* * *

Master are you content… with the time we present
Calling all to lament… to keep alive, your flame?
To some, it means nothing… holding a gathering
Just for remembering… the letters of your name
As we call the people… watching their tears trickle
And all of this while… loving you brings us blame
We took this blame as pride… everything we defied
Even if we had died… we loved you without shame

Hussain we saw your story… was worth not just life, but death
When death came to us it heard… your name spoken in our breath
In life or death, every path to you leads
Hussain extends his hand and intercedes

* * *

Master, you see a road… that leads to your abode
Upon it blood has flowed… of those who have no fear
Tell me O' generous… which of them is precious?
They walk a road vicious… just to upon you peer
Your help they have foretold… which of them will you hold
And into your wings fold… their dreams and wishes hear?
How beautiful is it… that this world they'd forget
So that when death they've met… to them you would appear

How beautiful is each walk… that it comes with one request
They came to you in this world… so rescue them in the next
The thirst of those with nothing your hand feeds
Hussain extends his hand and intercedes

* * *

Drawn deep within the eye… your dome beneath your sky
Watching seven skies cry… a sea of tears of blood
No-one it should surprise… that men learn from these skies
And with your day's sunrise… your lovers' blood would flood
All the tears that we've wept… the grief, on which, we've slept

BEGINNING & END

O' beloved, accept… these acts for our beloved
All this for you is praise… in yearning of your gaze
Hoping, in our last days… by you we'd feel loved

The eye that cries for Hussain… puts toward you a question
Is it wrong that every tear… requests from you salvation?
Those who saw his praise as the best of deeds
Hussain extends his hand and intercedes

* * *

In life you're medicine… soothing both pain and sin,
And when death is written… for you your lovers seek,
When I'm dressed in that shroud… when your love made me proud,
Buried before a crowd… placed on that dust, my cheek,
All that for you I'd done… wishes that you would come,
When I lie there alone… for you I remain weak,
Just as your hands lifted… all pains on us weighted,
Will we be comforted… when upon death we peek?

When our souls from bodies rise… let it them fall into your hand
Let the little that we did… be enough to by you stand
Just as in life for you each lover pleads
Hussain extends his hand and intercedes

* * *

(London – 22/08/13)

Revolution in the Heart
(In lamentation)

In every heart, Hussain has a revolution

* * *

I speak to you of a love greater than love
He falls a dreamer's falling star from above
And he perches upon the heart like a dove
His wings like the daybreak, around it open

* * *

His love is no legend, nor is it a myth
Though of a household of gold he is the fifth
He captures millions on his fortieth
Just ask them how by his love they awaken

* * *

Though for freedom within a battle he fought
Of an internal revolution he taught
The perfection of man selflessly he sought
A free world in each of us was his vision

* * *

His tale is much more than a mere story
It has treasures in it that lead to glory
And he who knows Hussain does not know worry
The answer to each worry he's been given

* * *

There is no-one who achieved what he achieved
For he challenged death, and death he then deceived
Now people of all ages for him have grieved
Where can you find such love and dedication?

* * *

Over one-thousand years and how they still mourn
As if he died yesterday, grief they adorn
With the dawn of his day, every heart is torn
The heart struggles with each pulse and contraction

* * *

A love such that builds a crown out of its pride
Telling the world that Hussain, his death, defied
They say he's dead, it answers he never died
And he's the crown on the head of creation

* * *

Open your eyes and give your pupils consent
You'll see him in every uprising present
You'll see him when the oppressed fight a tyrant
You'll know where to see him upon reflection

* * *

A love yearned by the biggest, greatest of kings
Every man longs for a place on Hussain's wings
Everything, its sorrow, for his tale sings
His hardship is his lover's tribulation

* * *

He is loved by even his own enemies
Swords against him, but his love in hearts won't cease
Gambling with his love, they do as they please
Spending his tragic day in celebration

* * *

It is not something small, to know of his name
Or to flutter like a moth within his flame
The only love where your actions, none would blame
For his love itself is a resolution

* * *

(Istanbul – 28/11/12)

Changing of the Flag
(In lamentation)

The month of sorrow on the horizon peers
The dark shroud of grief in the skies appears
Gathered in mourning are family and peers
As an immortal tale we remember

They world watches as they come to change his
Flag from red to black, just like the moon changes
Its colour from white to red, changes
The comfort of the eye to weep tears

Every eye weeps the absence of its beloved
The night sees the sadness of its beloved
Can someone left so alone be loved
So much that his love tears up every lover?

Tonight flags of black are raised on all shrines
In mourning Karbala recites, she rhymes
Her poetry in every heart shines
As every eye turns to look at Karbala

And with her we bear the weight of grief, a weight
And wait mere hours to mourn Hussain, a wait
That every lover dreads yet awaits
The wait of a servant to mourn his master

The flag of black, a symbol, they raise
Every ounce of desire, sin, it would raze
To the ground for it emits rays
Of light that burn the sins of every sinner

And with that we welcome… the month of Muharram

* * *

(Karbala – 14/11/12)

Take Me
(In lamentation)

Someone take me to Karbala... someone take me to Karbala
I want to speak to Hussain... I want to speak to Hussain

* * *

I've been living within a dream... because of it, daily tears stream
Every time I ask to visit... further away Karbala seems

How often I speak to my Lord... and how rivers my tears have poured
O' Lord take all you want from me... all I want is to him be called

All I want... is to return
All I want... is to see him
All I want... Hussain I yearn

I want to visit my Master... I want to visit my Master
I want to speak to Hussain... I want to speak to Hussain

* * *

I turn and I see everyone... telling me to Karbala come
But he hasn't invited me... and he's invited everyone

I keep waiting for an invite... every day with patience I fight
It tells me Hussain's forgotten... with my tears a message I write

O' Hussain... I am ready
O' Hussain... am I worthy?
O' Hussain... don't you love me?

For how long have I been waiting... for how long have I been waiting
I want to speak to Hussain... I want to speak to Hussain

* * *

Someone see how much I'm crying... someone see how much I'm praying
You all go to visit Hussain... and alone here I am staying

Is there some way to come with you... I promise I won't bother you
I'll even bring with me a flag... when we get there I'll pray for you

> Beside you... please let me be
> Beside you... let my eyes see
> Beside you... him before me

I beg you if you are going... I beg you if you are going
I want to speak to Hussain... I want to speak to Hussain

* * *

Your eyes shall be seeing his shrine... I have only tears inside mine
Every day I see you smiling... it kills me every single time

I'm happy that you are going... but I can't stop my tears flowing
Can I sit patient in this world... when to Heaven you are going?

> Tell Hussain... how much I'm hurt
> Tell Hussain... that we're apart
> Tell Hussain... I'm torn apart

And I'm still dreaming of his shrine... and I'm still dreaming of his shrine
I want to speak to Hussain... I want to speak to Hussain

* * *

At his grave I want to kneel... at his grave I want to wail
At his grave I want to tell him... how this world has made me feel

But I swear, every bit of pain... for everything that I'd complain
Everything would have been worth it... if I could just speak to Hussain

> And today... I am still here
> And today... everyone's there
> And today... I'm shedding tears

All I wanted was to visit... all I wanted was to visit
I want to speak to Hussain... I want to speak to Hussain

* * *

(London – 14/12/12)

BEGINNING & END

If You Visit
(In lamentation)

If you visit… I welcome you
And shall visit… each one of you
I will welcome those who visit, I will welcome
To you I'll come when you're buried, to you I'll come
If you visit

* * *

I was raised in a house of giving and service
My visitors should feel at home, I know this
I smile when I see my grave receives a kiss
And I'll make sure that when he leaves, Hussain he'll miss

If visited… it's my duty
I've awaited… those who know me
They've come and gone, and I serve them, they've come and gone
To you I'll come when you're buried, to you I'll come
If you visit

* * *

If a stranger comes to me, know I befriend them
If an orphan comes to me, know I father him
When someone comes to mourn me, I sing him a hymn
I brighten the hopes of he whose future seems dim

I'm a beacon… for the restless
For me they yearn… their lives I bless
The old and young, I assist them, the old and young
To you I'll come when you're buried, to you I'll come
If you visit

* * *

When you visit me, your life to me you've given
I care not for your sins for they are forgiven
You've risked death because you saw my shrine as Heaven

I adore you all who by my love are driven

If you love me... me you adore
Understand me... I love you more
Just as you've done I'll give you all, just as you've done
To you I'll come when you're buried, to you I'll come
If you visit

* * *

Come and visit me if this world has made you weak
Come and visit me if your desires you seek
I know what's in your heart but what to hear you speak
When you request from me, let tears flow down your cheek

I want to see... you in despair
So you love me... when I answer
What's on your tongue, I shall grant you, what's on your tongue
To you I'll come when you're buried, to you I'll come
If you visit

* * *

If you tire of me, than visit my brother
He jumps when he hears coming is Hussain's lover
I promise all your requests he shall look after
Visit him once for me, it'd be an honour

Abbas and I... servants truly
We'll bid goodbye... a safe journey
Do not be long with your return, do not be long
To you I'll come when you're buried, to you I'll come
If you visit

* * *

As you request from me, I have but a request
And I always remind each visitor and guest
If you want to visit me, remember this first
I came to quench your thirst when I was killed in thirst

And remember... when you come here
In Karbala... I was killed here

BEGINNING & END

If you are one, that remembers, if you are one
To you I'll come when you're buried, to you I'll come
If you visit

* * *

(Najaf – 14/11/12)

Forty Days
(In lamentation)

Forty days and counting... Karbala we're coming
Walking because in our eyes he is priceless
Walking because anything else is worthless

* * *

His fortieth comes and the Heavens hear a call
Descends on Karbala each lover and angel
The father leaves behind his wife, children and all
The mother carries the children that barely crawl

Men swear by their women... women by their children
No death on this road will bring to us distress
Walking because anything else is worthless

* * *

Descends on her dust every nationality
The only language that of lovers of Ali
The father tells the son, "get dressed and get ready
Forget your nation, today you're Karbalaei"

Every road to her bends... the millions descend
No fear, almost in the face of death, careless
Walking because anything else is worthless

* * *

The call of the man of serves Karbala's water
"Drink Abu Ali's water and curse Harmala"
Fatima watches, of whom do we remind her?
Qassim, Layla, Abdullah and Ali Akbar

Both the young and the old... every hand her hand holds
She breathes breath into the one who is breathless
Walking because anything else is worthless

* * *

He who serves us food, who does he see behind him?
He sees on his feet, pouring the food is Qassim
When they reach Karbala's border, who welcomes them?
Abbas cries out, "O' servants of Hussain, welcome"

His brothers by his side… his mother cries in pride
"Abbas bring me one of their children to kiss"
Walking because anything else is worthless

* * *

When to carry her child, she is unable
The mother pulls her son in a makeshift cradle
The old who can't walk as they legs are unstable
Finds their wheelchairs pushed by all those capable

Both the rich and the poor… walking to the same door
All one, he who is poor finds himself needless
Walking because anything else is worthless

* * *

I see a young girl and a flag she is holding
She reminds me of Ruqaya, I start crying
I see a woman, at the roadside she's standing
She reminds me of Zainab for Abbas waiting

She stands there, all alone… cries even hearts of stone
The tears that flow watching these things are endless
Walking because anything else is worthless

* * *

Upon this road whilst walking, I learnt a lesson
Never look back when Hussain's your destination
I have Hussain, therefore nothing else is my concern
Be by me or don't be, to my beloved I return

Catch up or lag behind… by Hussain, me, you'll find
My life belongs to him, he isn't worth less
Walking because anything else is worthless

BEGINNING & END

* * *

When with the millions on his grave I descend
I'll say I walked all this way to on you, peace send
The beauty of this walk only you comprehend
And I will return each year until my life's end

Till I'm old and frail… I'll walk on this trail
Yearly in the dress of death, for you I'll dress
Walking because anything else is worthless

* * *

London – 08/08/13

BEGINNING & END

The Road to Karbala
(In lamentation)

Karbala... Karbala... Karbala, your Lord drew you upon every eye
Karbala... Karbala... Karbala, your name flows with every tear and cry
Karbala... Karbala... Karbala, I give you a present with my life
Karbala... Karbala... Karbala, so on the Day of Judgement my head will be high
O' my Lord grant for me Karbala... I ask you by the greatest martyr

* * *

How much I've been dreaming... daily my heart's screaming Hussain
My eyes are begging me... saying, we want to see Hussain
My feet they keep walking... thinking they'll be reaching Hussain
My body's calling you... it comes running to you, Hussain

Karbala... Karbala... Karbala, you've stolen my body away from my mind
Karbala... Karbala... Karbala, till I see you I'm walking deaf and blind
Karbala... Karbala... Karbala, I give you a present with my life
Karbala... Karbala... Karbala, so on the Day of Judgement my head will be high
O' my Lord grant for me Karbala... I ask you by the greatest martyr

* * *

Far away from his dome... yet home is by his dome, Hussain
I leave with him, my heart... when from him I depart, Hussain
I step over death's head... and through death I shall head, Hussain
Your shrine is worth my death... your name worth my last breath, Hussain

Karbala... Karbala... Karbala, even death shakes when I mention your name
Karbala... Karbala... Karbala, because even the dead walk calling Hussain
Karbala... Karbala... Karbala, I give you a present with my life
Karbala... Karbala... Karbala, so on the Day of Judgement my head will be high
O' my Lord grant for me Karbala... I ask you by the greatest martyr

* * *

They told me, come walking… Master, I came running, Hussain
I set out on this road… and by you I'm shadowed, Hussain
When I cry and tire… Abbas gives me power, Hussain
When I feel alone… Zainab's shadow I'm shown, Hussain

Karbala… Karbala… Karbala, they speak of your wonder and beauties
Karbala… Karbala… Karbala, yet I relive a thousand tragedies
Karbala… Karbala… Karbala, I give you a present with my life
Karbala… Karbala… Karbala, so on the Day of Judgement my head will be high
O' my Lord grant for me Karbala… I ask you by the greatest martyr

* * *

When finally I see… Heaven infront of me… Hussain
I'll cry "peace upon you"… and I'll give my soul to Hussain
I gave all to visit… but it'll be worth it… Hussain
For I know when I die… I'll be visited by Hussain

Karbala… Karbala… Karbala, I'll thank you when I stand next to Hussain
Karbala… Karbala… Karbala, for my return in your sand I'll write my name
Karbala… Karbala… Karbala, I give you a present with my life
Karbala… Karbala… Karbala, so on the Day of Judgement my head will be high
O' my Lord grant for me Karbala… I ask you by the greatest martyr

* * *

(London – 10/10/12)

Nothing Will Stop Me
(In lamentation)

If my legs fail me... I'll throw them away...
Nothing will stop me from reaching Hussain walking
I want the world to see... the flag I carry...
Nothing will stop me from reaching Hussain walking

* * *

Against the Earth's turn... millions return... and return walking...
To their beloved
A revolution... against oppression... what an uprising...
They have created
Returning to him... the road salutes them... the skies envy them...
By angels guarded
The flags that flutter... touch the hereafter... and by the Lord's throne...
Each of them greeted

Beneath their feet hell shakes... the dead in envy ache...
Nothing will stop me from reaching Hussain walking
Their lives are all stake... all for their beloved's sake...
Nothing will stop me from reaching Hussain walking

* * *

What an uprising... with the sun's rising... Hussain calls for help...
Millions reply
With them the sun sets... the moon by them rests... the tents on the route...
Like stars in the sky
The widowed women... hold orphaned children... "children, if we die...
Don't let Hussain die"
Oppression topples... walks with them, angels... the death of Hussain...
Millions defy

For something that's priceless... all else is valueless...
Nothing will stop me from reaching Hussain walking

Every soul is selfless… against danger, heedless…
Nothing will stop me from reaching Hussain walking

* * *

Leave everything… don't bring anything… leave and start walking…
Heaven is calling
The Day of Judgement… watches this moment… it descends on Earth…
And it starts walking
Don't bring your worries… your calamities… just hold up a flag…
The world is watching
If you have a wish… carry your anguish… Hussain is watching…
Abbas is listening

Leave everything behind… the road to Hussain find…
Nothing will stop me from reaching Hussain walking
Make sure your will is signed… leave a mark on mankind…
Nothing will stop me from reaching Hussain walking

* * *

I see the world shakes… when a man's heart aches… he stands there begging…
"Please let me serve you
Do not walk by me… come rest beside me… you visit Hussain…
I know your value!"
Millions become… a flag of freedom… and with their walking…
Redefine virtue
Heaven it descends… the road with them bends… the blessings with them…
if only they knew

So why are you waiting?   When Heaven's awaiting…
Nothing will stop me from reaching Hussain walking
Get up and start walking… every soul is going…
Nothing will stop me from reaching Hussain walking

* * *

(London – 24/11/13)

BEGINNING & END

Karbala's Month
(In Celebration)

This is Karbala's month... Hussain born on the third
Born on the fourth, the moon... the fifth Imam Sajjad
This month, Karbala glows... in awe of its heroes
Abo Sajjad's Sajjad, Hussain and his brother
Two suns and a moon make this month like no other

* * *

Welcomes Sha'baan, Karbala... lit up in pride and honour... for its loved ones
She leaves in awe, each lover... each man wants to be with her... and she listens
She decorates her wonder... on her beauties, men ponder... her sand sweetens
She perfumes each visitor... leaving the hearts so tender... for three lions

Leaving all within her crush... smitten by a city lush
For three names, a lover's hush... she listens
Her best, Karbala shows... In awe of its heroes

* * *

On this month's third, we attain... the prince of Heavens, Hussain... as he's born
His birth shakes each tyrant's reign... upon each tyrant's domain... freedom drawn
A rise that none can explain... Hussain's name none can contain... this newborn
His love glows within the vein... and his love none can restrain... we're reborn

God blesses this rising sun... as Zahra adores her son
A dress of freedom, golden... he had worn
In fear, Karbala's foes... In awe of its heroes

* * *

This month's fourth would reveal... a moon, yet one so surreal... this, Abbas

His body made of steel... by the father of zeal... none could pass
In service he would kneel... with his eye on his heel... none surpass
Teaching, Hussain's his seal... and Hussain's greatness he'll... teach his class

Only with his brother's birth... was known this Abbas's worth
To him this is Hussain's Earth... lakes and grass
In love, Karbala grows... In awe of its heroes

* * *

Only few board Hussain's ship... fewer know Sajjad's worship... to his Lord
His tongue with God, he'd equip... words that rested on each lip... souls would board
From worship's beauty he'd sip... on divine beads, hold his grip... his soul soared
On this day, beats of hearts skip... as the balance of kingship... is restored

Prayer's a crown of gold we wear... but Sajjad beautifies prayer
A status no-one, nowhere... can afford
Karbala tears its woes... in awe of its heroes

* * *

Karbala, rise up in your pride... two suns and a moon reside... in your land
Mortality they defide... with the battle-cries they cried... proud you stand
Your beauties, tonight, don't hide... these three, none can, if they tried... under¬stand
Tonight hearts to you are tied... their tears of joy they have dried... with your sand

Every soul is left in awe... from the eye tears of joy pour
Millions of hearts implore... from your hand
Dreams to Karbala flow... In awe of its heroes

* * *

(London – 15/06/13)

THE GUARDIAN OF THE VEIL

Poetry in memory of the Father of Virtues (pbuh)

"No I do not care if they say it's impossible
You are the Abbas, you make anything possible"

BEGINNING & END

In Awe of You
(In lamentation)

I see you Abbas as the crown that sits on my head
And your name it flows beautifully in each tear it shed
All are… in awe of you
Abbas… I adore you… in each tear I shed

* * *

O' immortal flag that against the wind flies
O' mountain that alone could hold seven skies
O' who could not bear to hear those children's cries
I tell you that your name, Abbas, never dies

Generations sit, and in awe of you, they listen
And your name sparkles in the tears that, on them, glisten
Watch them… they ache for you
Abbas… I adore you… in each tear I shed

* * *

O' diamond that your virtues found and made rare
O' he who has left souls frozen by his glare
O' he who cares for those that are without care
You have hearts knocking on your door everywhere

All of your father's lovers share an understanding
If they have a need, at your door they will be standing
Knocking… waiting for you
Abbas… I adore you… in each tear I shed

* * *

O' lion that, waiting to serve, would kneel
O' volcano that erupts with your zeal
For you, standing with no water was surreal
O' Abbas we know you and know how you feel

You stood there confused, as the water poured to the ground

Every drop that falls came for you a torturing sound
Confused… we witness you
Abbas… I adore you… in each tear I shed

* * *

You loved them so much it was almost unfair
Your eyes would light up and burn with their despair
Who hurt them, your thunder would burn out their air
Bodies for these girls' tears, to you it was fair

Your heart had a gate, and no-one would dare open it
These girls had a key, they'd come and, inside your heart, sit
Their touch… it comforts you
Abbas… I adore you… in each tear I shed

* * *

You reshaped love and you called it brotherhood
Yusuf wishes that, in Hussain's place, he stood
O' flagbearer have you not yet understood?
Even love would sing your praises if it could

Don't you understand, O' highest peak of selflessness?
You are a symbol to oceans of hearts in distress
Are you… aware of you?
Abbas… I adore you… in each tear I shed

* * *

After you, we found no battle difficult
And to no stranger have we bowed down or knelt
If we were ever weak, your anger we felt
In Abbas's flame, all those who oppressed would melt
In every lover O' Abbas there is a battle
And from what you've taught, to win it, we are capable
In us… we all found you
Abbas… I adore you… in each tear I shed

* * *

With your sweet name, my existence I would crown
I adore your smile as I do your frown

BEGINNING & END

You taught me to raise my head up when I'm down
Because when I look up, there I see your crown

Everything you are and stood for, it became my pride
I recall this pride with every tear I try to hide
I crowned… my head with you
Abbas… I adore you… in each tear I shed

* * *

If you see that within sorrows I'm drowning
Won't you extend your hand, after everything?
If I tell you "Abu Fadhil, I'm begging…"
Would you turn away and leave this heart breaking?

No I do not care if they say it's impossible
You are the Abbas, you make anything possible
In need… I come to you
Abbas… I adore you… in each tear I shed

* * *

(Dallas – 20/05/13)

The Moon Descends
(In lamentation)

The sky to water bends... the moon here it descends
Upon the Earth descends the moon, and it looks at the river
I've torn the skies to come to you, and bring those children water

* * *

On that day the river saw a miracle
As the moon descended upon the battle
He'd see mothers, their thirsty children cradle
They would cry "thirst" if to cry they were able

These children were the stars... the moon upon them stares
They cannot speak from such a thirst, the moon glows red in anger
I've torn the skies to come to you, and bring those children water

* * *

I'm the moon and I saw standing the princess
In her royal eye I saw drawn her distress
She gazed at me as the peak of selflessness
The impatience of her thirst, her eyes confess

I saw thirst within her... I turned to the river
I'm the father of all zeal, and thirsty is my sister
I've torn the skies to come to you, and bring those children water

* * *

I am the moon and I saw alone, the sun
Begging for water, surrounded him children
He tells them, O' children helpless don't become
Be patient with your thirst as soon death shall come

When I heard the word death... I then swallowed my breath
Every eye turned toward the flag, and turned toward its bearer
I've torn the skies to come to you, and bring those children water

NOURI SARDAR

* * *

Today the moon descends upon this desert
Left enraged by every child's discomfort
O' river my throne in the sky I'll desert
To kneel to each child and soothe their thirst

River, let your heart sink... from my hands they shall drink
Let them sip from my hands or you'll sip from the sword of Haider
I've torn the skies to come to you, and bring those children water

* * *

The enemy watches the moon by the tents
And a promise to the stars, the moon presents
For him to collect water, the sun consents
Every enemy's mother for them laments

They know they'll meet their end... when the moon, the sun sends
And charges toward them the moon, screaming out all his valour
I've torn the skies to come to you, and bring those children water

* * *

Charges the moon, flashes from his sword thunder
Either they bleed or from his sword they scatter
It's the moon in battle or it is Haider
The red sea parts for the moon in Karbala

Just to run for the moon... they jump into their tombs
Beneath the ground, they hear his voice, no lightning, only thunder
I've torn the skies to come to you, and bring those children water

* * *

Beside the river the moon, alone, stands tall
Each drop of water its gravity would pull
If for the return of its water it calls
Abbas won't take a little, he'll take it all

The river shakes in fear... from it, its water tears
Just as death calls those children's names, I came to hear your despair
I've torn the skies to come to you, and bring those children water

BEGINNING & END

* * *

The moon cries out and his cry shakes the battle
Death runs to him and with death the moon wrestles
But death deceives him and his hands it grapples
And with his flag and water, the moon topples

No-one for the moon cares… the stars for him despair
Of a failed promise, this dying moon is the carrier
I've torn the skies to come to you, and bring those children water

* * *

(London - 17/12/12)

BEGINNING & END

Water I Threw Away

(In lamentation)

I remember / in Karbala / O' Haider
This flagbearer / for his brother / O' Haider
Water today / I threw away / O' Haider

* * *

I recall as but a young boy… your death left wounds O' my father
And around it I built a wall… of zeal, courage and honour
It hurt me that you sat bleeding… and kissed both my hands O' Haider
You placed in one hand a canteen… and a flag within the other

It was written / for your children / my slaughter
Never hidden / for your Hussain / my slaughter
My own safety / I threw away / O' Haider

* * *

Riding out to the land of death… I watch Zainab in her grief stand
I recall when you took her hand… and placed it firmly in my hand
I make a promise to myself… as the men of courage I band
I won't let fear approach her heart… even if blood pierces this sand

No-one comes near / or leaves in fear / my sister
On death I peer / and hold her near / my sister
My night and day / I threw away / O' Haider

* * *

I stood at the edge of the tents… watching as the women would mourn
And saw Habib coming to me… between love and sorrow he's torn…
He tells me, "I have a story… in my aged eyes, it is still drawn
Your father told me that to die… tomorrow, Abbas, you were born"

This is my fate / a title great / a martyr
The night is late / on me a weight / a martyr
Doubt and worry / I threw away / O' Haider

* * *

Was I raised in such a manner… that from thousands I'd run away?
A sight I see ignites my eyes… Ali's children crying "thirsty"…
I take my flag & take my sword… watching their lives in my hands sway
My fortitude like a mountain… and no river stands in my way

In me a flame / and I became / like Karrar
A lion's name / that none could tame / like Haider
Yazid's army / I threw away / O Haider

* * *

I watch the dust as it rises… and mixes with enemy blood
A mirror of you O' Karrar… their bodies for all that I've loved
I do not care about death's grip… and with my sword through death I flood
The way I sail through these men… they think I'm you O my beloved

I hear them cry / this is the eye / of Badr
Bodies, they fly / beneath the sky / of Badr
The enemy / I threw away / O' Haider

* * *

With the scent of death on my hands… I reach the river in sorrow
I raise water to take a sip… and watch it between fingers flow…
The sweetness of the water near… I watch it both glisten & glow
I recall Hussain and those girls… from my hands, the water I throw

In thirst they sink / I will not drink / the water
Tearless, they blink / they speak and think / the water
Water, they'll say / I threw away / O' Haider

* * *

I ride out back toward the tents… feeling the wind brisk through my hair

And feel as my hands are cut… the grip of those children's despair
An arrow hits me, I can't see… but I don't stop, nor do I care
Till an arrow hits the canteen… And I lose all that I held dear

The hopes I had / to quench their dread / would shatter

BEGINNING & END

I feel my head / with blood it bled / would shatter
Hope, as I lay / I threw away / O' Haider

* * *

(London - 22/11/13)

Abbas-Ali

(In lamentation)

Who is it that's angry?   Abbas or it's Ali

* * *

Who is it, that flashes from his sword thunder?
Every flash reveals the hero of Badr
From the charging moon like cattle they scatter
This is who his mother had named him Haider

From one they run away   Abbas or it's Ali

* * *

His battle-cry, mountains would hear if they could
His voice tears their eardrums like fire on wood
This is my Khandaq and this is my Uhud
These girls are Muhammad, you're my Ibn Widd

Which lion wants its prey?   Abbas or it's Ali

* * *

He charges, a ship through soldiers left adrift
The river's my Khaybar and its gate I'll lift
I am Abbas and I've been given a gift
In battle, like my father, through death I drift

Whose is this voice, really?   Abbas or it's Ali

* * *

Run or stand in awe and bask at my marvel
My sword thirsts for your heads with the ground level
This is Karbala and this is my Jamal
Today I'll cut the legs off Yazid's camel

Which one's sword is thirsty?   Abbas or it's Ali

* * *

This is Sofeen and I picture an image
Its ink like fuel that flows to ignite my rage
They held Qurans on spears, you hold Hussain's age
Since birth I've been chained but you've rattled my cage

Who to charge is ready?   Abbas or it's Ali

* * *

He tears his roots, toward the river he leaves
His sword tears apart waves of bodies like leaves
Each enemy's mother for their child grieves
Through Abbas's blood the blood of Ali weaves

Anger of him heavy   Abbas or it's Ali

* * *

Is the zeal of Ali, Abbas reliving?
Or is the lion in my brother living?
Are they both returning, or are they leaving?
For which one will, alone, Zainab be grieving?

She weeps a tragedy   Abbas or it's Ali

* * *

(Orlando – 31/08/13)

This is the Farewell
(In lamentation)

This is the farewell... you're future I tell
Abbas Abbas Abu Fadhil

* * *

Come to me, my son... for the time has come
For the moon to rise... and to die, the sun
Make me a promise... never forget this
Do not be scared if... you're too hands I kiss

Kissing them and a sight I remember
I recall when your hand clenched my finger
Abbas make a promise to your father
And give both hands away to your brother

Abbas, promise me... give both hands away
Abbas Abbas Abu Fadhil

* * *

Promise me Abbas... brotherhood surpass
Toward your brother... by you let none pass
Remember Badr... Uhud remember
Show them that you are the son of Haider

Your soul to Hussain's forever is bound
I always found you where Hussain I found
Abbas plant your flag deep within the ground
Your head O' my son with Hussain I've crowned

Your brother defend... your life to him lend
Abbas Abbas Abu Fadhil

* * *

I leave you three things... your flag, your name sings

And for your two hands... I leave you two wings
With the childrens' cries... let me see you rise
Show them even death... the Abbas defies
I'd glow with pride when I'd see you kneel
A pride my son's the father of zeal
I raised you so that fear you'd not feel
Abbas rise and with the devil duel
Show them that you are... the son of Haider
Abbas Abbas Abu Fadhil

* * *

Your fate I picture... my eyes they captureSuch a sacrifice... that my hands nurtureAbbas your story... will bring you gloryWhen that sweet water... your hands throw away
There will not come for you a greater dayEnemies beyond time watch in dismayAnd my lovers when to the Lord they prayWill ask by he who water threw away
This promise I make... for you, hearts will shakeAbbas Abbas Abu Fadhil

* * *

(London 30/07/13)

Just Forget Me
(In lamentation)

Just forget me… just forget me… and bear my absence O' mother of tragedy
Just forget me… just forget me… because I know hurt you will every memory

* * *

It has all passed… and in your past… you walked away from me lying by the river
And in your head… voices taunted… saying he does not recall you, nor does he care
How much it must have hurt you to walk away
When you were so used to me crying out "stay"

Don't think of me… don't recall me… for I won't be there to ease your calamity
Just forget me… just forget me… because I know hurt you will every memory

* * *

I know your gaze… into my eyes… wanted to soothe every pain and all my worries
I know it hurts… but you should know… that it was only your sight that brought to me ease
And now I sleep with an arrow in my eye
And no hands that will come and all your tears dry

Don't expect me… don't await me… I have left all that I've loved for the Lord's decree
Just forget me… just forget me… because I know hurt you will every memory

* * *

Upon my chest… you left your tears… a place for your tears on my
shirt I had promised
But this promise… I've broken it… and left in a moonless night all that
I once missed
And if you want your two eyes dried when you're alone
Forget of my hands and dry them with your own

Do not hate me… just forgive me… because I won't forgive myself for
your worry
Just forget me… just forget me… because I know hurt you will every
memory

* * *

I'm a mountain… you're a fountain… when you were hurt this
mountain would crumble and fall
And if a wound… upon me loomed… your fountain would topple and
your water would fall
So forgive me if when you're struck I turn away
And forgive my severed hands for making you cry

Do not let me… hear you need me… for I can't come running and it'd
destroy me
Just forget me… just forget me… because I know hurt you will every
memory

* * *

(London – 02/12/12)

If Abbas Sends Back Your Wish
(In lamentation)

If Abbas sends back your wish… I'll close my pen forever

* * *

If you have a problem, hardship or a wish
Ask he who in helping those girls would flourish
Let the soother of their thirst soothe your anguish
Trust my ink and trust its words… to your plead his eyes wander

* * *

The door of Abbas for wishes is well known
At his door wishes like roses have been thrown
Every rose into a granted wish has grown
Send him a rose, it returns… as a bundle of flowers

* * *

When you find your heart on a hopeless road stands
To he who has no hands extend both your hands
Don't fear to knock his door for he understands
Abbas no request burdens… raised in the house of Haider

* * *

If your find your wounds of grief like rivers bleed
Turn to Karbala and say "Abbas, I plead"
Ask him by Zainab he will intercede
If you're a woman, ask more… for you'll remind him of her

* * *

If impossible tasks upon your road lie
Find a flag of Abbas, on it a knot tie
Tell Abbas, I've asked and await your reply

Don't think, ever, he'll ignore… not when you've tied his banner

* * *

If you're by the grave that all his lovers crave
Take a scarf and throw it on-top of his grave
You'll see give you he who two hands away gave
Don't stay in your fear or doubt… speak to Hussain's flagbearer

* * *

Hold the bars that shrine his grave and with tears speak
Whisper the dreams of your heart, tears on your cheek
In his two hands lies all that you want and seek
Don't be afraid, speak your heart… you can trust Hussain's brother

* * *

If Abbas denies your wish, I'll stop writing
And make sure my poems they stop reciting
This is Abbas, impossible is nothing
If Abbas lives, then he hears… and remains the best carer

* * *

Tell him, Abbas, I ask by those children's thirst
By the soldiers who argued who would fight first
By the child whose blood from his small neck burst
By Qassim, your brothers and… your nephew Ali Akbar

* * *

(London – 27/08/13)

Under the Care of Abbas
(In lamentation)

The orphan with no father… the stranger with no carer
All find themselves looked after… under the care of Abbas

* * *

Since the day yearned the lips of Abbas that sweet water
Any thirst yearning to be quenched yearns Hussain's brother
Anything held by his hand in its pride would flutter
Ask the flag that was comforted by its flagbearer
Against every wind it flies… knowing in whose hand it lies
Impossible that it dies… under the care of Abbas

* * *

It wasn't just for a day that to cries he'd listen
In any voice that cries for help, he hears those children
We see the moon against its own orbit has risen
And see the wishes in our hands his hands have given
Against what's impossible… of miracles capable
Able is the unable… under the care of Abbas

* * *

Could it be that the Abbas is our biggest secret?
No hardship falls on us before with him it has met
If any doubt his power, tell them, lest they forget
The moon defeats the sun daily with every sunset
A secret only we know… and in secrets it would glow
Testifies the tears that flow… under the care of Abbas

* * *

Even the flag of Abbas today sings his praises
If it flies against the wind then the wind's flow changes
In his name the written and unwritten it judges
And the care of his lovers beneath his flag passes
In itself Abbas it brought… his every notion and thought
Whoever has tied a knot… under the care of Abbas

* * *

Not a saint whose name has died or lives within legend
He lives in the flutter of his flag, until time's end
Neither are his hands severed, our pains with them he'd mend
And the scale of what's possible his name would bend
In the eyes of death he peers… and his glare even death fears
Those who love him, find their years… under the care of Abbas

* * *

To the voice of his brother daily he'd awaken
"O' my brother, after you my back has been broken!
"O' moon in your absence I witness my nights darken
My daughters not by thirst but by your absence shaken
The cries of my children… asking when will he return
Brother, all their protection… under the care of Abbas

* * *

(London - 06/12/13)

THE MOTHER OF CALAMITY

Poetry in memory of Zainab (pbuh)

"Her shrine it bends the scales against all mankind
Man is man, but Zainab, she is one of a kind"

End of Times
(In lamentation)

Could it be the end of times?   Look at the crimes... against her
They have their eyes on her shrine... and her bloodline... defend her
A message we've given... we are Zainab's children

* * *

I arose in painting a rose, Ali's daughter
I wanted to paint a picture, and I picked her
For this there was none worthier, and none worth her
But not as we stand with her, I watch her wither
This is who if men discuss her, it disgusts her
A sister of the moon asks, who will assist her?

I have painted a picture... and I brushed her... with sadness
The mother of tragedy... so silently... in distress
On this canvas, written... we are Zainab's children

* * *

She saw they were coming for her and for her throne
The princess of calamity from her throne, thrown
I heard the screaming of this rose, she's all alone
And her screaming sounded like the crushing of bone
If they dug up her grave and they reached her tombstone
For the sin that shakes the heavens can they atone?
If they take out her body... and take, proudly... her captive
What excuse to her father... and her brother... can we give?
Can we let it happen... we are Zainab's children

* * *

I felt as if I stood at the edge of time's end
And standing here, I saw upon Zainab a trend
I felt that with a tyrant she had to contend
And that a captive to Kufa, Zainab they'd send
Only now there'd be not a soul to, her wounds, mend
With her between their hands who will, to her wounds, tend?

If her body is taken... she'll awaken... between them

For us she will be searching… and complaining… against them
In her eyes, her vision… we are Zainab's children

* * *

Oppression wanted a grave and Zainab's they find
The stand against oppression, alone, she defined
The beauty of her dome makes them, with anger, blind
God bless the hand that, her golden palace, designed
Her shrine it bends the scales against all mankind
Man is man, but Zainab, she is one of a kind

Her shrine, it is a beacon… nations listen… to her voice
In the eye, her dome glistens… the heart weakens… without choice
An easy decision… we are Zainab's children

* * *

A call came that froze the blood deep within our veins
We will not rest till not a single grave remains
Is it the devil that's holding Syria's reigns?
Is it Zainab captive, or her father in chains?
They destroyed Hijr's grave and wanted his remains
How long before their eyes will turn upon Hussain's?

No we will not allow them… we're the children… of zeal
The devil's hand will never… her shrine, enter… and feel
As dark shadows widen… we are Zainab's children

* * *

I saw, high on her dome, her brother's banner flies
Even after her death, her flowing tears, he dries
The name of Zainab on their forehead, each man ties
This pride we've marked upon our heads, it never dies
Know that by the grave of Zainab, our pride, it lies
It will manifest into Mehdi if she cries

God forbid, if she topples… evil grapples… with Mehdi
Just as the sun is rising… his uprising… eyes will see
He knows if he'd return… we are Zainab's children

* * *

(London – 21/05/13)

By the Blood of Hussain
(In lamentation)

By the blood of Hussain... we will always remain
The name Yazid will never last... your name none will remember
The name Zainab will always last... and it will last forever

* * *

To Yazid they bring Ali's daughter captive
The anger of Fatima they all relive
Don't think to her, permission to live, they'd give
It was Zainab that allowed them all to live

She breaks apart her chains... and her voice is Hussain's
They let her speak, and with her tongue... Umaya she would slaughter
The name Zainab will always last... and it will last forever

* * *

She speaks, knowing her words will never fail
It's as if Haider's hiding beneath her veil
Don't think after Karbala she was frail
Her words like arrows upon Yazid hail

She tears apart his throne... and scares him to the bone
Hussain returns with his revenge... in the voice of his sister
The name Zainab will always last... and it will last forever

* * *

The sword of Ali descends upon her tongue
She fears nothing except the Lord who is One
O' Yazid, you let her speak, what have you done?
If she raises her hands, help you will no-one

At her words, mountains fall... tyrants, to her, they crawl
Daughter of Safa and Marwa... and they shake at her anger
The name Zainab will always last... and it will last forever

* * *

In her shadow they see her father appear
I'm the lion that all other lions fear
When I'm angry the angel of death will hear
And you're holding my brother's head on a spear

Listen to me, I swear… your soul, apart, I'll tear
I hold your soul within my hand… if I want, it will shatter
The name Zainab will always last… and it will last forever

* * *

Understand when I say if I give the call
From the sky the moon upon your head will fall
If I wanted, to my feet I'd make you crawl
Your life, your throne, your palace, I'd take it all

My uncle is Hamza… my father is Haider
The backs of their heads, they had eyes… to them armies surrender
The name Zainab will always last… and it will last forever

* * *

I swear by the stars, the skies and by my Lord
Till the Day of Judgement we will be adored
Don't think you killed us when Hussain's blood, you poured
Today my brother's blood defeated your sword

My brother never dies… and soon Mehdi will rise
Do not think that death will save you… your bodies he'll recover
The name Zainab will always last… and it will last forever

* * *

(London – 19/05/13)

I See

(In lamentation)

I see... the sun setting infront of me
I see... the moon setting infront of me
I see... not day or night, but your bodies... I see

* * *

I was left alone and I saw the sun setting... how upsetting... I see this sight
And all I've known is when it sets, I'm left greeting... the moon's sighting... I see this sight
Yet today's sunset with the moon is not meeting... what a painting... I see this sight

Tell me... does the sun set, and never rise?
Tell me... does the moon abandon the skies
Tell me... for both my brothers my heart cries... I see

* * *

In the absence of light I stood in a darkness... and so restless... I'd cry
their names
Whenever hurt or danger my eyes would witness... or in sadness... I'd
cry their names
And I could not search for, without the sun's brightness... the moon's braveness... I'd cry
their names

I seek... I cry rivers, for my brothers
I seek... the sun to dry out these rivers
I seek... the moon, on his helmet feathers... I see

* * *

I looked everywhere for the moon, even the night... was without
light... without the moon

Me and the skies would feel safe, but with his plight... we live in fright... without the moon
I'd recall him upon his horse, beaming moonlight... O' what a sight... without the moon

I wept... hoping that he'd come when he hears
I wept... hoping that he would wipe my tears
I wept... and I waited decades and years... I see

* * *

I asked to see the sun and saw it was laying... and I'm praying... O' what a sight
Alone and for my brother's warmth I was craving... how amazing... O' what a sight
And yet hanging from his horse I saw him swaying... and not moving... O' what a sight

I screamed... seeing the sun on earth fallen
I screamed... as witnessed by all his orphans
I screamed... knowing that he won't awaken... I see

* * *

When taken captive for the sun and moon I'd plead... that my road leads... to see their light
I yearned to by those who destroyed them out of greed... be let go, freed... to see their light
I returned to hear the sun and moon were carried... to be buried... to see their light

I stood... in neither the day nor the night
I stood... in grief's darkness, without their light
I stood... I witnessed the sun and moon's plight... I see

* * *

(London - 08/11/12)

In A Poem
(In lamentation)

The sun rises to Karbala's silence… and it comforts the mother of patience
And in a poem Zainab and the sun converse

* * *

The mourning… the sun sees scattered bodies in the morning
The morning… cannot handle seeing Zainab in mourning
The mourning… the mourning of Zainab upsets the morning
The morning… complains to the sun of hearing her despair

The cry from her, it wakes up the sun… it rises to find beside her, no-one
Her cries recite to the sun her troubles in verse
And in a poem Zainab and the sun converse

* * *

Just ahead… the sun wakes to see her standing just ahead
Just ahead… she points to her brother's body just ahead
Just ahead… no brother, and upon a spear, just a head
Just a head… is what they called I when raised upon a spear

The sun on a spear and the sun watches… to be the head on the spear it wishes
The severed head of Hussain, his enemies curse
And in a poem Zainab and the sun converse

* * *

So aware… Zainab, I'm of your tragedy, so aware
So aware… today I dressed myself red, and so I wear
So I wear… this colour to show you that I'm so aware
So aware… of the bodies and tears that are scattered here

When between bodies I saw that you stood… the weight of your sorrow I understood
And the flags of my grief to the world I disperse
And in a poem Zainab and the sun converse

* * *

Every tear… reminds me of what my eyes saw, every tear
Every tear… his neck severed, demolished me every tear
Every tear… I would scream, hearing the sound of every tear
Every tear… would be slow because taunting me was Shimr

His neck severed, Hussain lay there helpless… the blood of his neck, it became his dress
Itself into my brother, his sword would immerse
And in a poem Zainab and the sun converse

* * *

He remains… in my voice and in my actions, he remains
He remains… but I cannot bear looking at his remains
His remains… I've drawn a picture of grief by his remains
His remains… they cry this is all that's left of your brother

You rise up and bring me another day… when for my death, all my sorrow would pray
Between his death and my life, I don't know what's worse
And in a poem Zainab and the sun converse

* * *

(Karbala – 29/12/12)

I Remembered Zahra

(In lamentation)

When I saw the tents burning with fire
I remembered the house of my mother
Alone in Karbala… I remembered Zahra… I remember

* * *

The tents ablaze and alone here I stand… with no-one left to embrace
As both my feet are being burned by the sand… and fire scorches my face
Today someone else's pain I understand… today her steps I retrace
They did not find a Zahra upon this land… so I have taken her place

There was no house of Fatima to burn
So they burned all the tents of her children
On each child, a scar… I remembered Zahra… I remember

* * *

When I heard Hussain to Abbas crying… "Brother my back is broken"
I remembered the sound of something breaking… when Zahra's rib was taken
When I saw him from the river returning… looking pale and shaken
I remembered by Zahra he'd be wailing… "O' mother please awaken"

I remembered Hussain upon her chest
When Shimr upon my brother would rest
And I screamed from afar… I remembered Zahra… I remember

* * *

When I heard Hussain's child crying from thirst… "O' father I am thirsty"
I remembered the child who before birth… cried "mother please protect me"
When the veins of Abdullah's neck would burst… and I saw a killed baby

I remembered the one who me this death first... before his cradle would
sway
One soon after his birth met with his death
One met his death long before his first breath
In my shock and horror... I remembered Zahra... I remember

* * *

When I was alone and I faced danger... I cried "help me O' Abbas"
I remembered your voice crying for Haider... when your chest nails
would pierce
And just like into our house O' my mother... these oppressors would
trespass
Through the tents, defenceless, with no protector... hundreds of Shimrs
pass

I curse the one who crushed you with the door
Hundreds just like him into our tents pour
With arrows and fire... I remembered Zahra... I remember

* * *

O' Zahra around your daughter this world burns... and this fire has no
end
The one who burned your house with fire returns... and your daughters
I defend
I watch the smoke as into my lungs it turns... the ashes toward me bend
A Fatima Zahra Yazid's army yearns... curses upon me they send

I remembered when I smelt the ashes
Your chest O' Fatima the door crushes
And I scream O' mother... I remembered Zahra... I remember

* * *

A daughter in distress yearns her mother's arms... in your absence I wail
I wanted your hand but found blood on my palms... and it came from
the nail
O' Fatima your voice comforts and it calms... my torture to you I tell
You bid farewell to me and your absence harms... when to all I bid
farewell

I was tortured by the tears in my eye

BEGINNING & END

When to every loved one I bid goodbye
Between dead I wander… I remembered Zahra… I remember

* * *

(London – 19/03/14)

THE IMMORTAL DAY

Poetry in memory of the family and companions of

Imam Hussain that were martyred or left in loss on the day of Ashura (Peace be upon them all)

> "We saw his blood was worth more than the greatest gold
> And all riches are outweighed by Hussain's household
> The care of his daughters into our wings we fold
> And their right to water with our swords we uphold"

Will I Recall You?
(In lamentation)

Will I picture you O' father… in my head, in my head
I've already drawn you in the… tears I shed, tears I shed
Hear the words of an orphan… you leave behind your children
I've already drawn you in the… tears I shed, tears I shed

* * *

My eyes gaze upon your face… and your features they retrace
And if I forgot your beauty… what memories would I embrace?

Father, know in your absence… no hand shall soothe my grievance
No hand to wipe the tears I shed… or soothe me with its presence

If I must live an orphan… I'll draw my father often
With my own tears of grief as ink… and my wails as my pen

When in sadness I will draw you… O' father, O' father
And remember that I was once… your daughter, your daughter
My wounds shall remain open… you leave behind your children
I've already drawn you in the… tears I shed, tears I shed

* * *

I asked you before you left… father, do orphans forget
What their father looks like, tell me… for this alone I have wept

Before you left O' father… did you not once but ponder
Are fatherless children kept safe… by the world that they wander?

I'm scared, if they struck your head… and Hussain, rivers you bled
What will they do to his children… father, my future I dread

I know, that if hurt, I'll cry out… your sweet name, your sweet name
And recall the times I was hurt… and you came, and you came
To me running you would come… you leave behind your children
I've already drawn you in the… tears I shed, tears I shed

* * *

I hold you, and you hold me… by the warmth of your body
My heart flutters in its comfort… nothing but beauty I see

Do you know what your warmth brings… I feel an angel's wings
Protecting me, like a mountain… lullabies to me it sings

Torn from me is this fortress… and it leaves me in distress
And if a daughter is distressed… she awaits her father's kiss

All I expect from you father's… a cuddle, a cuddle
And if you want, your daughter you… can cradle, can cradle
My comfort became a dream… you leave behind your children
I've already drawn you in the… tears I shed, tears I shed

* * *

Father, I've lost all patience… I can't live in your absence
You hear your daughter's heart breaking… yet remain at a distance

Father, my heart is breaking… father, my soul is screaming
We were like one, and you left me… your daughters heart is aching

For your daughter do you care… of my grief are you aware?
Can my name from your memory… away, so quickly you tear?

In all this I'm still trying to… remember, remember
How you looked like, how you once were… a father, a father
I wish that your face I'd drawn… you leave behind your children
I've already drawn you in the… tears I shed, tears I shed

* * *

(Karbala – 16/11/12)

Kufa to Karbala
(In lamentation)

In Hussain's eye a tear... farewell my messenger,
From Mecca to Kufa... it ends in Karbala

* * *

Hussain cries out O' my cousin what game has Kufa played?
O' writers of Kufa upon my household's blood you wade,
In my eyes if he is preyed on, then on me you have preyed,
And if he sways from his horse it's as if the world has swayed
His Lord his only companion, and after he had prayed,
He turns his head and sees behind him, no helper, no aid

He calls out for Hussain... Hussain's tears of blood rain
Written is the future... it ends in Karbala

* * *

Alone in the city and if he finishes his prayer
The only support left for him sleeps in his eye, a tear
Even if he turns his head and all helpers disappear,
Kufa's mosque and sky and desert cry O' Muslim we're here
Yet his hope flickers when only silence reaches his ear
No friends, and no family, only enemies appear

He reads Falaq and Nas... his sword cries O' Abbas
And he begins the war... it ends in Karbala

* * *

He rises and refuses to be his own tragedy
And within him ignites the blood of Khaybar's family
His allegiance and his zeal is a thing of beauty
He draws his sword and begins the battle with "O' Ali"
An army of angels behind him, tell me who's lonely?
One man, fed Badr from his cradle, against an army

Written upon his palm... Ali's my first Imam
And I'm his defender... it ends in Karbala

* * *

Muslim battles alone yet the hundreds he endangers
If ever he tires then Hussain alone he pictures
O' Bani Umaya I'm of Bani Hashim's soldiers
The son of Abu Talib to no tyrant surrenders
Is this all that you have brought me? Bring me greater numbers!
And the heads of disbelief the sword of faith dismembers

Muslim upon his sword... Shi'i on the blood poured
In Kufa lives Badr... in ends in Karbala

* * *

They take Muslim to Ibn Ziyad and he's wrapped in chains
O' Muslim where are your supporters? Not a soul remains
Know that our tyranny shall hold Iraq's neck by its reigns
And once we have taken your life we will go for Hussain's
If from giving allegiance to us your cousin refrains
We'll add his children's lives, his women captive to his pains

To Hussain say goodbye... in tears of blood you cry
His cries the skies will hear... it ends in Karbala

* * *

(London 08/11/13)

BEGINNING & END

The Angel of Death in Kufa

(In lamentation)

The angel of death for me came… in Kufa he calls out my name
And if he returns my soul to my creator
I'm scared he'll then search for Hussain in Karbala
In Kufa he calls out my name

* * *

I am Muslim and I have a pledge with Hussain
To gather support and topple a tyrant's reign
They wrote to us, of this tyranny they'd complain
Forbidden on us to from requests abstain

We are the house that grabs the hand… of any who struggle to stand
Tell the angel of death I have a duty here
I'm scared he'll then search for Hussain in Karbala
In Kufa he calls out my name

* * *

O' angel of death when for any soul you call
They answer you, at your feet even tyrants fall
Where's I'm left no assistance, left me them all
And as upon my head calamities befall

Seventy-one are with Hussain… with me not even one remains
If the angel of death knows I've no supporter
I'm scared he'll then search for Hussain in Karbala
In Kufa he calls out my name

* * *

I walk alone, no supporter, from street to street
The angel of death calls out 'Muslim, your death greet'
I feel the clutch of failure upon my heartbeat
Because of me, will Hussain face a harsh defeat?

O' angel of death let me stay… for more support I swear I'll pray

For if this angel takes me to the hereafter
I'm scared he'll then search for Hussain in Karbala
In Kufa he calls out my name

* * *

It may be so, that with martyrdom I'm fated
But my reply, my master, Hussain's awaited
By the picture of Hussain killed I am haunted
And so by your coming O' death I am taunted

To Hussain I have a duty… this shapes my content as mighty
If I accept death my fortitude shall wonder
I'm scared he'll then search for Hussain in Karbala
In Kufa he calls out my name

* * *

They tell me drink before we throw you to the ground
Each time I sipped, in this cup my own blood I found
I gaze to the land of death to which Hussain's bound
O' Hussain the world has your cousin abandoned

Only the angel of death knows… what hardship throughout my blood flows
No, it's not because death or martyrdom I fear
I'm scared he'll then search for Hussain in Karbala
In Kufa he calls out my name

* * *

(London – 30/07/12)

The Ansar
(In lamentation)

Our bodies are not worth more than our beloved
And our blood isn't worth more than Hussain's blood
Let our bodies on Karbala's desert rain
And be killed a thousand times, all for Hussain

* * *

We the Ansar, from near and far, came to his aid
He stood alone as Yazid's sword upon him preyed
Dare they touch him, when our souls by his feet we laid
His death is death, and life began when him we praised
All our souls cried, when with our eyes, on him we gazed
If they touch him, the Heavens scream, the Earth is swayed
The son of the Ka'ba and of Mohammed
Is worth our children crying and our blood shed
On our bodies we'll build a throne for his reign
And be killed a thousand times, all for Hussain

* * *

We came running when a lone cry had reached our ears
Alone he stood, in his heart grief, in his eyes tears
He cried out not knowing if any soul hears
"Is there any to help me as death on me peers?"
We told Yazid, take our bodies, our heads on spears
We told death to delay his death and take our years
We told the swords to upon our bodies prey
And for our beloved threw our lives away
And when killed we cried out again and again
And be killed a thousand times, all for Hussain

* * *

We saw his blood was worth more than the greatest gold
And all riches are outweighed by Hussain's household
The care of his daughters into our wings we fold
And their right to water with our swords we uphold
For something greater than gold our bodies we sold
The greatness of Hussain's love sleeps in swords we hold

Today for the greatness of Hussain we rise
Our bodies scattered with tomorrow's sunrise
For our murders none of us will dare complain
And be killed a thousand times, all for Hussain

* * *

We saw the worth of Hussain as something unreal
And with our blood, his loneliness we would heal
Today the greatest companions we'll reveal
No tents will burn, and no women shall they steal
Today we'll crush Yazid's army beneath our heel
And we'll make his army to our Hussain kneel

O' Yazid today is the Day of Judgement
And you'll regret making our Hussain lament
Let us defend him here on Karbala's plain
And be killed a thousand times, all for Hussain

* * *

(London – 06/11/13)

The Awaited Visit
(In lamentation)

Ali's beautiful name flows deep within the vein
A spring of which flowers near it never complain
O' Haider from our eyes our tears like rivers rain
We're the Ansar, and your absence, it brings us pain
When will the day come when we visit you again?
Will it be after we are killed for your Hussain?

Today our lives we shall give… just so that we can relive…

ت فوش ك ح يرض اي ردي ج .. ت فوش ك ح يرض

A sight that is expensive… its absence is destructive

ت فوش ك ح يرض اي ردي ج .. ت فوش ك ح يرض

ي حورب ك ت يرت شا .. لا ن ظت ك ت ي س ن

* * *

اي موي ف و شأك بات عأ .. ف قوأ ن يزح ك باب ب
عجراو ك روز أ اي ردي ج .. عجراو ك روز أ
ل وط ه ي لع ك باي غ .. ق ات ش م م شأك بارت
عجراو ك روز أ اي ردي ج .. عجراو ك روز أ
هن آت ي وهلا .. لا ن ظت ك ت ي س ن

* * *

O' Haider we've longed to see you for years and years
When we cried, the sight of your shrine flowed in our tears
Today for your Hussain we face arrows and spears
Hoping that when we die your shrine to us appears
Now that the time of death O' Haider to us nears
Will we see you? O' Ali death upon us peers

O' Haider are you listening… for Hussain we're battling

ل ك ي رك ف ك مي اي ردي ج .. ل ك ي رك ف ك مي

To the battle we're leaving… and of you we are thinking

ل ك ي رك ف ك مي اي ردي ج .. ل ك ي رك ف ك مي

ت شع ك ت ي ن ذ ث ب .. لا ن ظت ك ت ي س ن

* * *

You taught us O' Haider never to be oppressed
And all our swords against Yazid's hand we have pressed
Today in the armour of death we are all dressed
And our last wills to our families are addressed
We are proud but so many of us are distressed
It's been too long since with seeing you we've been blessed

How long has it really been… Ali when have we last seen?
قاتـ شمـكـ فوشأ ايـ رديـ جـ .. قاتـ شمـكـ فوشأ
O' Haider on hope we lean… still hoping in the unseen
قاتـ شمـكـ فوشأ ايـ رديـ جـ .. قاتـ شمـكـ فوشأ
امايـكـ تـ يخن .. لا ذظتـكـ تـ يـ سن

* * *

O' Haider for Hussain the blood of our veins flows
Seventy two, for him three-thousand we'd oppose
Every man cries your name before to war he goes
We'd die a thousand times for Hussain and he knows
The way you fought at Badr every man follows
Haider with our blood we'll start drawing your shadows

O' our beloved with our blood… we shall draw out our beloved
مـ سرأ كـ لايـ خ ايـ يـ جرد .. مـ سرأ كـ لايـ خ
As the arrows to us flood… we shall draw out what we loved
مـ سرأ كـ لايـ خ ايـ رديـ جـ .. مـ سرأ كـ لايـ خ
يـ حوربـكـ تـ يـ قل .. لا ذظتـكـ تـ يـ سن

* * *

O' Haider with our blood the sword we defeated
With our bodies the name of Hussain we lifted
When we're buried and with the dust we are greeted
We won't feel any pain or fear on us weighted
Because we'll see the sight that we have awaited
And cry finally his grave we have visited

And when we stand there we'll say… as from our crying we sway
ينزّيح كـ دعبـ ايـ رديـ جـ .. ينزّيح كـ دعبـ
Finally by you we pray… nothing can take it away

BEGINNING & END

بعدك حيرّني .. ج يردي اي بعدك حيرّني
سيدَ تظندُ لا .. ريتَ كترحمني

* * *

(London – 06/11/13)
Arabic verses by Jaber Al-Kadhemi

BEGINNING & END

Qassim's Request
(In lamentation)

O' youth hear me, my tragedy, when you mourn and rememberHear my story, hear my glory, and help me live foreverOn that day my uncle taught me… live like Ali, die like Hussain

* * *

O' youth when you recall me and for me weepThe lessons of my story in your tears keepI saw my uncle alone and wouldn't sleepI tell you, the tears he shed, angels would sweep
Feeling guilty, Ramla saw me take Hassan's armour and shieldShe cried for me, none could make me throw down my sword and yield I told my mother please let me… leave this tent and my death attainOn that day my uncle taught me… live like Ali, die like Hussain

* * *

O' youth know by two names I was left in aweI'm young, but I can't explain the things I sawFor years, for a man named Ali, tears would pourThe pride of his name, every man near me wore
I saw a pride that never died, we were the sons of AliIn awe of us, they all loved us, and this every day I'd see A promise that lived inside me… a pride my actions would maintainOn that day my uncle taught me… live like Ali, die like Hussain

* * *

I was young when they killed my father Hassan
Every eye would look at me as an orphan
All alone and came to wipe my head, a man
Now he's all alone and to help him I can

When I was young, to me he'd come, and he'd become my father
What has become, he has no-one, he's calling for a helper
What kind of son would Qassim be… if all alone he would remain?
On that day my uncle taught me… live like Ali, die like Hussain

* * *

I lived my life in my grandfather's shadow
From my morals my love for Ali, they'd know

And on that day, his words to the world I'd show
Yesterday has gone, uncertain's tomorrow

Work within this world, he would say, as if you'll live forever
And as if you'll die tomorrow, work toward the hereafter
Today's my day, I'll work for me…. to be known as "Qassim, the slain"
On that day my uncle taught me… live like Ali, die like Hussain

* * *

My uncle had a love of Ali so grand
For being his son, he was led to this land
All his sons, the name Ali, on their hearts band
He'd name all Ali, if he had a thousand

I saw Hussain, he loved this name, it left my uncle entranced
A young lion, I embraced him, and with this great name I pounced
Ali's zeal flowed inside me… I'd make the enemy's blood rain
On that day my uncle taught me… live like Ali, die like Hussain

* * *

My grandfather of this day, he was aware
He knew who'd die for Hussain and how and where
If he's watching, how can I into life stare?
How can I live if he wanted me killed here?

I left my tent, Ramla'd lament, by her cries to war I'm led
Her tears drip down… my wedding gown… to her nightmares I have fed
If fate wanted me to marry… I'd not have seen Karbala's plain
On that day my uncle taught me… live like Ali, die like Hussain

* * *

I'd cry out pretending my voice was thunder
I am the hero of Uhud and Badr
I'd pretend I was the one struck on Qadr
So young, but I wanted to be like Haider
So young and yet still they feared me, I hope my grandfather's proud
I imagined I was Ali, leaving, in awe, Badr's crowd
Ali, you're the father of dust… accept me as one of its grains
On that day my uncle taught me… live like Ali, die like Hussain

* * *

BEGINNING & END

O' youth on that day I learnt many lessons
And because of it my name in hearts glistens
When they realized I was of Hassan's orphans
Their sword called out my name and death, it listens
Swords cut through me, death embraced me, arrows at me they'd propel
I was murdered and massacred, I learnt this from my uncle And perhaps
Hussain learnt from me… like me, his throat cut vein to vein
On that day my uncle taught me… live like Ali, die like Hussain

* * *

(Istanbul – 20/12/12)

I Prepared Him Honey

(In lamentation)

I prepared for him honey... his body returned to me
Farewell O' my Qassim... farewell O' my Qassim

* * *

I lit for him a candle... whilst his horse he would saddle
A soldier, not a groom... a soldier, not a groom

* * *

I prepared ink for his hands... washed it, the blood of these sands
And with blood it washed him... and with blood it washed him

* * *

My face wanted a smile... this land wanted my wails
I sang a painful hymn... I sang a painful hymn

* * *

I had purchased for him gold... his gold to the swords he sold
And with it sold my dream... and with it sold my dream

* * *

I had chosen him a bride... he was her honour and pride
On her hopes his blood streams... on her hopes his blood streams

* * *

My candle, he had left it... and taken Hassan's helmet
And left my tears to stream... and left my tears to stream

* * *

Honey for Qassim I'd poured... he left it and took his sword
Off to death with a grin... off to death with a grin

* * *

(Karbala - 21/11/12)

BEGINNING & END

Goodbye Qassim
(In lamentation)

I saw him a moon, shining like no other
Handsome as he hides his tears from his mother
No longer a child… he'd make his mother proud… goodbye Jassim

* * *

I looked upon a sight and O' what a sight
I saw his face like the moon, drenched within light
A moon flickering as he welcomes his plight
He leaves his mother within a moonless night

O' child my nights are days in your presence
I will light candles just to fill your absence
To light candles she'd vowed… he'd make his mother proud… goodbye Jassim

* * *

I used to smile when to me you'd awake
And when you would sleep O' Jassim I would ache
I'd cry for your pain and smile for your sake
And now that you leave, every memory you'll take

You leave your mother as a child no more
Memories of your youth become for me, torture
Her heart, grief, would enshroud… he'd make his mother proud… goodbye Jassim

* * *

No it's not easy to bid my son goodbye
I've drawn your beauties on the lens of my eye
I adored you when from Ramla you were shy
I adore you now, as your youth you deny

I adore the rose that today holds a sword
The gem of my eyes that none else could afford

As to his youth he bowed… he'd make his mother proud… goodbye Jassim

* * *

Your age will not know how a heart is broken
I won't get to tell you with tomorrow's dawn
Know that it won't break, no, it would be stolen
Daily I'll search for it but you won't return

For a broken heart, every hour is late
There will be no Jassim to bear such a weight
And they cry out aloud… he'd make his mother proud… goodbye Jassim

* * *

Today, they see you, like a moon flickering
Since your birth O' Jassim, I've seen you shining
You leave and with you, your sword and helmet bring
And when you leave you take from me everything

Reach into my chest, and take from me my heart
With it take my soul, for now with it I part
He takes with him his shroud… he'd make his mother proud… goodbye Jassim

* * *

When you gifted to me years of your presence
Is it fair to torture me with your absence?
Your mother was crushed by mountains of patience
And beneath its weight, this queen calls for her prince

No-one came to lift it and to sooth my pain
I tried to gasp for air and drowned within rain
And tells her, every cloud… he'd make his mother proud… goodbye Jassim

* * *

(London – 18/05/13)

Stay

(In lamentation)

Stay... your mother wants you to smile
You leave her to cry and wail... stay

* * *

Qassim... I am your uncle and this is my battle
Qassim... tell me the yearning for death why do you feel?
Qassim... this is my tragedy, this is my trial
Qassim... don't let me hear another mother's wail

Stay... on me your mother's tears hail
You leave her to cry and wail... stay

* * *

Tell me... your eyes they see a path that before you beams
Tell me... is it your martyrdom or your mother's dreams
Tell me... for her emotions, what shall tomorrow deem?
Tell me... will tears of joy or of grief from her eyes stream?

Stay... her heart is caught in a gale
You leave her to cry and wail... stay

* * *

Listen... she's a mother and every mother's the same
Listen... every day, of your wedding your mother dreams
Listen... if this dream of hers impossible became
Listen... her heart would ache every time she heard your name

Stay... daily she'll recall this tale
You leave her to cry and wail... stay

* * *

Her heart... she entrusted to you, left it in your hands
Her heart... she gifted to you all its rivers and lands

Her heart… and slip through your hands would the grains of its sands
Her heart… so tell her why with no heart your mother stands?

    Stay… with the one who'd sway your cradle
    You leave her to cry and wail… stay

* * *

Her eyes… would wake in the morning longing for your sight
Her eyes… saw all as darkness but saw your face as light
Her eyes… yearned the comfort of your eyes when left in fright
Her eyes… for but a glance of you, the world they would fight

    Stay… without your sight, her skin pale
    You leave her to cry and wail… stay

* * *

Your eyes… the yearning for martyrdom in them I find
Your eyes… make me realise you won't sleep if left behind
Your eyes… looked like Hassan's eyes when with mine they aligned
Your eyes… and my brother's requests I've never declined

    Stay… or go and embrace this trail
    You leave her to cry and wail… stay

* * *

You go… wearing your father's armour and his turban
You go… whilst your mother prepares for you a coffin
You go… she throws away every marriage-thought and dream
You go… her dreams die and become her tribulation

    Stay… is something she cries out while
    You leave her to cry and wail… stay

* * *

(Istanbul – 13/11/12)

I Lament

(In lamentation)

When I let you go and your name I would call
Every moment you held me I would recall
Tortures me, every moment… and in your absence I lament… I lament

* * *

O' whose name sleeps in the deepest depths of my heart
My heart tortures me whenever we are apart
It would complain it's not complete, left it a part
And screaming your name to your mother it would start

And what should I reply to my heart's complaints?
The picture of my beloved to me it paints
Wounds to me it'd present… and in your absence I lament… I lament

* * *

Let me explain to you the heart of a mother
She sees none to the keys of her heart worthier
You slept deep in my womb and slept there no other
And there daily, my heart your two hands would smother

It was there you drew your name upon my heart
If I part with you, then from my heart I part
You stole it without consent… and in your absence I lament… I lament

* * *

You held me and for a last time, you I'd cuddle
I recalled when I'd cuddle you in your cradle
I wondered if to forget you I'm capable
To picture you till my dying days I'm able

I kissed your forehead, upon your face, my tears
Every tear asks what could become of your years

My heart plummets in its descent… and in your absence I lament… I lament

* * *

Today a man, when once with my hand, you I fed
And your name slept in every single prayer I read
I tell you as upon our last moments we tread
It was a pride to have a son like Mohammed

I put my soul in your hand and bid farewell
The pains of your absence to my nights I'll tell
Memories of you abundant… and in your absence I lament… I lament

* * *

They say that Heaven lies beneath a mother's feet
I say I smelt Heaven's scent when you I would greet
Where goes the one whose absence his presence would treat?
My love, I hear calling your name my own heartbeat

Have you not seen what my tears draw when they flow?
In yearning your comfort they draw your shadow
My heart is perfumed by your scent… and in your absence I lament… I lament

* * *

You leave the tent and my heart becomes like this tent
Yearning for you, in love with you, but you're absent
I feel the weight of every second and moment
And I break down, and for you Ali I lament

You leave and I feel fall, my heart's pillar
From its fall, I feel my own soul shatter
Severs my dreams, every fragment… and in your absence I lament… I lament

* * *

In my final hopes O' beloved, my hands I raise
Yearning for one last glimpse of my beloved's gaze
For returning Yusuf to Yaqub You I praise

BEGINNING & END

O' Lord to my painful nights return my sun's rays

O' Lord he who returned Yusuf to Yaqub
My grief challenges the patience of Ayoub
Prophets are mourning my torment… and in your absence I lament… I lament

* * *

Today O' my beloved I've sold my hopes to fear
I welcome old age and watch death upon me peer
What a tragedy, when I hope that you'd appear
I see the rose that I've raised, raised upon a spear

Praying every day that death would welcome me
So in death I'll see welcoming me, my Ali
And my heart to you I'll present… and in your absence I lament… I lament

* * *

(London – 06/10/13)

For What Sin?
(In lamentation)

He cries… for what sin did my child die?
He cries… and throws his blood toward the sky

* * *

This is the father who today watched his son… massacred as a child in his two arms
The tears of thousands of Prophets in his eyes… and the blood of Mohammed stained on his palms
Feeling the arrow, he waves his tiny arms… and the voice of his father no longer calms
The eyes of Hussain blinded before his death… watching as his young child, an arrow harms

He cries… why does my child from me shy?
He cries… and throws his blood toward the sky

* * *

This is my child, six months, what was his sin… it tortures me to see my child thirsty
I forget my own thirst and only saw his… upon my beloved the pangs of thirst would prey
Yet for all the pain I had seeing his thirst… soaked in blood, I can't see my child this way
With an arrow in his neck, in my wails… my beloved to death's hands I gave away

He cries… lifeless, why does in my hands lie?
He cries… and throws his blood toward the sky

* * *

Every father overjoys with his son's birth… and I wonder if my enemies have sons
What father, evil or good can bear the weight… of knowing that his infant, murdered, becomes

If me and my brothers were of Hashim's moons... then our sons within our eyes were truly suns
The weight of losing a son matches the weight... of the weight of happiness when a son comes

He cries... and all fathers to his grief cry
He cries... and throws his blood toward the sky

* * *

Abdullah, you sleep in secrets of my heart... whoever knows my love for you, knows Hussain
I find the gaze that once brought my heart comfort... now brings my heart nothing but the chains of pain
With no brother, son, nor a friend to complain to... I throw your blood to the sky and I complain
And when I fall beside all that have fallen... I'll watch it return when from skies, blood shall rain

He cries... tears that draw Asghar in his eye
He cries... and throws his blood toward the sky

* * *

Lord, I hold this lifeless child in my hands... my stand against this tyrant I have fulfilled
When they look back at this day, they shall all ask... for what sin was Hussain's young infant's blood spilled?
With my child's blood, I've defeated the sword... tomorrow by millions he shall be held
And whenever they hold a child, they'll cry... Hussain's beloved infant in his arms was killed

He cries... to his son, a final goodbye
He cries... and throws his blood toward the sky

* * *

(London – 10/10/13)

BEGINNING & END

To Najaf I Turn
(In lamentation)

O' my grandfather... I miss my father
To Najaf I turn... ask him to return... I miss my father

* * *

I am Ruqaya O' Ali your grandaughter
I have no father so help me O' grandfather
I ask as a daughter who misses her father
Don't I need a father to be called a daughter?

Alone, so confused... all else I've refused
Only him I yearn... ask him to return... I miss my father

* * *

I was taught from birth that Ali brings miracles
Calls your name every tear that from my eye trickles
With your arm raise the Khaybar's gate of my trials
Return my father and his smiles and cuddles

The gate of Khayber... my grief's heavier
And its weight it burns... ask him to return... I miss my father

* * *

"Mohammed's the sun, Ali's the moon" I was taught
O' Ali between the day and night I am caught
I wake yearning him, I wake crying and distraught
At night I can't sleep because he's my final thought

Cries for me the moon... my days in ruin
From me sorrow learns... ask him to return... I miss my father

* * *

I can't ask my aunt: tell me where my father went?
Whenever I asked, she'd turn her face and lament

Bring him to me, I don't need anyone's consent
I am a daughter who misses her father's scent

I miss his smiles… I miss his cuddles
Tell them my concern… ask him to return… I miss my father

* * *

Why don't you answer me, would you turn me away?
I'm still that daughter that beside your grave would play
My skin is pale, from ashes it has turned grey
Ali maybe you don't recognise me this way?

It's me, grandfather… give me an answer
Don't leave me to mourn… ask him to return… I miss my father

* * *

I refuse to let my tongue touch the word "goodbye"
I miss his figure drawn on the lens of my eye
For years your grey beard, Ali, you refused to dye
If I must wait years, from this sorrow let me die

Not another day… take my soul away
A painful pattern… ask him to return… I miss my father

* * *

I slept and I saw my beloved when I slept
I held Hussain's chest and upon his shirt I wept
He told me, from me, for too long you have been kept
I woke and I screamed, and from my chest my soul lept

Thankyou O' Ali… he came back for me
Gone is my question… ask him to return… I miss my father

* * *

(London - 03/12/13)

THE SYMBOL OF PATIENCE

Poetry in memory Lady Ummul Baneen

(Peace be upon her))

"You are the son of Ali, he's the son of Mohammed
You're the hands, he is the eyes, I am the tears that he's shed"

Gave Away My Hands
(In lamentation)

You are the son of Ali, he's the son of Mohammed
You're the hands, he is the eyes, I am the tears that he's shed
I gave away my hands… he gave away his hands

* * *

I see the moon in front of me, it is crouching
To quench its thirst or stay in thirst it's deciding
It turns to me and says, mother, are you watching?
How can I drink when for water the sun's waiting?

If he is the eyes, I know he is watching from his tent
If I am the hands, water from my hands I must present
Would he think, on these sands… he gave away his hands

* * *

I tell him, son, he is the sun, he is the eyes
You are his hands and you must wipe the tears he cries
And if he falls, to break his fall, his hand it tries
You are his hands and this duty in your hands lies

A duty that I have whispered to you from your cradle
I gave him a pair of hands to assist him in battle
So that he understands… he gave away his hands

* * *

They wanted hands and I gave them only a pair
But I gave them away without shedding a tear
If from your arms, O' my beloved, you two hands tear
Know that for him, I gave my hands without a care

Remember your mother if your hands are torn from your arms
And I shall remember my fingers were clenched by your palms
Upon faraway lands… he gave away his hands

* * *

You are the hands, he is the eyes, but what am I?
You shall find me in every tear the eye would cry
I'm the shadow of his sorrow, don't ask me why
You see him hurt, your mother's hurt, let your heart die
I raised you in such a way, that you're the father of zeal
If he's in pain then I'm in pain, and pain you would feel
If your zeal disbands… he gave away his hands

* * *

If you're in thirst, remember first, that he's thirsty
You are his hands, water in his hands let him see
Do not dare drink, his thirst and not your thirst hurts me
O' my son the water in your hands throw away
Fill up that canteen with water and return to Hussain
Even if you die from thirst, don't let thirst with him remain
And if thirsty he stands… he gave away his hands

* * *

If to the tents with the water, Abbas, you ride
Know that they shall come attacking from every side
When an arrow within your eye, it shall reside
And your hands tear, only then I shall have my pride
And even when you lie meeting your end upon the ground
I want to hear "O' brother forgive me" as your last sound
Your absence he withstands… he gave away his hands

* * *

London – 09/12/12

All of My Sons
(In lamentation)

All of my sons... for Ali's sons
I tell my Lord whenever to Him I pray
I am the mother who gave her sons away

* * *

I'm a mother who has a pride and what a pride
I'm the lioness who gave away all her pride
In the love of Mohammed, daily, I'd abide
I gave everything and in my Lord I relied
I had a voice that like Ali's battle-cry cried
With my four children's lives, Yazid's rule I defied
I shook his throne... with every son It is the pride that lives with me every dayI am the mother who gave her sons away

* * *

How many doors God opens when one door opens
I married Ali and raised for him, four lions
Each one holds each other's back and holds their burdens
And in the love of Hussein, their bond, it strengthens
They are all but presents to the prince of Heavens
And I'd give them if they were four or were thousands
Since they would crawl... I gave them all I did not allow a single one to stay
I am the mother who gave her sons away

* * *

I gave birth to each son and beside each cradle
I'd sing them lullabies and each son I'd cradle
In each lullaby, a lesson to them I'd tell
You are all mortal, but Hussain is immortal
Do not ever let him from his sorrow tremble
When he draws his sword, infront of him assemble
His sorrows mend... his life defend I'd tell my children when in my arms, they'd play
I am the mother who gave her sons away

* * *

My grandfathers for wrestling with lions were praised
And for my beloved Hussain, four mountains I raised
They gazed into his eyes before in mine they gazed
They saw the beauty in his eyes and were amazed
Every day upon Karbala's dust they all prayed
Knowing that, just to die for Hussain, they were raised
I would not cry… knowing they'd die I raised them knowing that they would die someday
I am the mother who gave her sons away

* * *

I tell my Lord, you've given me such an honour
I sacrificed so Hussain can live forever
And I make a promise to you O' Creator
If any serve Hussain, their names I'll remember
If they ask me for a wish then I shall answer
To every lover of Hussain, I'm a mother

If they love him… they're my children I will rescue them, if in their grief, they sway
I am the mother who gave her sons away

* * *

In the absence of them all, for death I've waited
I raise my hands, even though with grief they're weighted
O' Lord, death, for years and years, I have awaited
This is the tongue that for your Hussain recited
Take my soul and with death, let my soul be greeted
Allow me to with Hussain be reunited

Just for his sight… give me my plight
Toward my beloved son, show me the way
I am the mother who gave her sons away

* * *

London – 12/04/03

Alone

(In lamentation)

Alone... is what they call me when they see
Alone... Ummul Baneen without sons she's
Alone... not even a shadow with me... alone

* * *

I have slept countless sleepless nights, only the stars... provide me light...
without my moons
And in the dimness of my nights, I cry a scream... and no-one hears...
without my moons
Within the darkness of these nights, my wounds, they bleed... and are
not healed... without my moons

I weep... Only the stars witness my tears
I weep... Living in night for days and years
I weep... Not a moon to comfort my fears... alone

* * *

I recall when if I was scared, they'd coming running... hearing my cries...
at my service
Now every day I live in fear and not a soul... comforts my heart... at my
service
Now at night even my shadow leaves me alone... no longer there... at my
service
My house... Was once raised by many pillars
My house... Only beauty in its mirrors
My house... Fell with Abbas and his brothers... alone

* * *

Within the absence of light what does one become... let me tell you...
I'm so alone
When light is dim, I'm left speaking to my shadow... and it tells me... I'm
so alone
When there's no light, I'm left drawing, my sons shadows... and they tell
me... I'm so alone
Shadows... Are all I know of happiness

Shadows... Draw out for me my memories
Shadows... Remind me that I am son-less... alone

* * *

Know that the word, goodbye, is harsh upon my tongue... and when you're gone...
I draw the moon
To pretend that my son Abbas is still with me... in his absence... I draw the moon
I sent him to battle as if I don't love him... yet when he's gone... I draw the moon

He left... and saw not a tear in my eye
He left... not knowing how much I would cry
He left... thinking I'm smiling, he would die... alone

* * *

If I want to speak the words that within my heart... rest there, so deep... I'd recall him
I'd recall when his tiny hands clenched my finger... and I'd smile... I'd recall him
But when left overjoyed by this bundle of joy... I'd see Hussain... I'd recall him
I'd see... memories of me telling them
I'd see... I told them I'd sacrifice him
I'd see... that one day in my house I'd dream... alone

* * *

When I hold his children and I see them smile... I'd recall him... I'd faint and fall
If they looked thirsty, I would first look for Hussain... he'd not be there... I'd faint and fall
And when I'd fall I'd wait for him to pick me up... where was he when... I'd faint and fall

Abbas... I have blocked your name from my mind
Abbas... your soul to Hussain I'd assigned
Abbas... but when I'm hurt, your name I find... alone

* * *

(Karbala – 09/12/12)

Called Me Ummul Baneen

(In lamentation)

I wish they never called me Ummul Baneen
I raised five sons and not one would remain
Where are her sons? No Abbas and no Hussain
No Abdullah and no Jafar... no Uthman, son of Haider

Not a son beside me, only memories
When I see my shadow, Hussain my eye sees
Let me see them just once before I die, please
Let me, just once, sit with them... let a mother see her children

Tell me, how patient can a mother's heart be?
'Ummul Baneen' and yet not a son with me
A mother without sons, what a tragedy
A tragedy drenched in my tears... and I live it for months and years

I see them coming to Medina just ahead
I see Zainab and Um Kulthoom just ahead
But Hussain has no body, just a head
And his body lies fallen in Karbala

I'm left complaining to no-one and nobody
I cry out and comes to help me, nobody
I just see Hussain's head and no body
They tell me my son's head was raised on a spear

* * *

Remember Her
(In lamentation)

Remember her… she's the mother… of Ashura… Ummul Baneen
The first to cry and mourn… from her servants are born… Ummul Baneen

* * *

If your eyes have ever shed tears… whenever to you reappears…
The image of Ashura
The image of heads upon spears… the little girls drowned in their fears…
And the mourning of Zahra
And whenever Muharram nears… in every mosque a name appears…
Alongside every lover
When you mourn it is she who hears…. to mourning she gave all her years…
This is Abbas's mother

When we're mourning… and lamenting… by us, crying… she's always been
In her chest, her heart torn… from her servants are born… Ummul Baneen

* * *

She raised and gave away four lights… a moon and stars that lit her nights…
Not one by her would remain
Her pride writes and her soul recites… the flame of love in her ignites…
"May my sons for him be slain"
Her patience it had reached such heights… she did not care for her sons' rights…
Yet for Hussain her tears rain
On a title she set her sights… one that in her sons' blood she writes…
"The first servant of Hussain"

What a promise… a sacrifice… at what a price… like none have seen

To give her sons, she'd sworn... from her servants are born... Ummul Baneen

* * *

Remember and never forget... the mother who made her suns set...
Is the reason that we're here
Long after Ashura's sunset... alone at Baqi she would sit...
Telling all what happened there
She's the mother of this pulpit... she would recite with her eyes wet...
And hearts, in two, she would tear
Without her, mourning, none would let... and no chest by hands would be hit...
For Hussain none would despair

All is from her... this reciter... these words you hear... all from this queen
In tyrants' eyes, a thorn... from her servants are born... Ummul Baneen

* * *

A promise from this small servant... in our lives, in every moment...
Ummul Baneen's a blessing
If you want something that's absent... go and ask her, don't be silent...
And she'll give you everything
Even if, to be, it's not meant... don't think that she can't or she won't...
Something better she will bring
If a mother four moons is sent... and these moons to death she'd present...
Impossible is nothing

If you want proof... then ask yourself... how I myself... paint you this scene
Her miracles we've worn... from her servants are born... Ummul Baneen

* * *

What hatred and what oppression... her dome by rubble is hidden...
No minerets and no gold
By her no commemoration... no servants, no tents are open...
No mourning, no flags are held

It's because they fear her lesson… one thousand years, yet she glistens…
Her power it is untold
I don't think with grief she's stricken… she'll give her grave like her children…
So yearns Hussain's grave, the world

"Four sons I gave… give me no grave… Karbala crave… visit Hussain My Hussain I adorn"… from her servants are born
Ummul Baneen

* * *

(London - 08/02/14)

THE IMMORTAL GUIDANCE

Poetry in memory of the Imams of the Holy Household

(Peace be upon them)

> "After his death we saw the last glimmer of day
> As Monsoor cries "no more Shia after today"
> Indeed since that day our freedom was locked away
> Till our only hope was to for a return pray"

Let Me Show You Jaber

(In lamentation)

Jaber visits Karbala whilst old and blind
Grief grips his heart and sorrow torments his mind
He hears a man digging, who does Jaber find?
Alone weeps Imam Sajjad   By the grave of his father

* * *

He asks Sajjad, O' Master what happened here?
Why do I find Hussain's grave wet with your tears?
Why do I hear that heads were carried on spears?
Sajjad takes his hand and weeps   Let me show you O' Jaber

* * *

He speaks to Jaber and his voice is shaken
Jaber over here the Ansar were taken
And no-one was left to protect the children
Hussain stood crying their names   And none of them would answer

* * *

Over here the women cry, do you hear them?
O' Jaber here they massacred our Qassim
A young boy and the swords towered over him
With armour too big for him   We brought him to his mother

* * *

A body looks like Mohammed or Ali
Jaber here Ali Akbar was killed thirsty
And within his father's arms he passed away
Who brought him water at last?   Mohammed and Fatima

* * *

Did Abbas clench your fingers when he was born?
O' Jaber here I saw the moon's arms were torn
Yet only when he lost water he would mourn
With no flag and with no arms   I buried the flagbearer

* * *

O' Jaber don't ask why I returned in dread
I have returned to return my father's head
O' Jaber his grave weeps from the blood he's bled
When I buried him he cried   Bring to me Ali Asghar

* * *

(London - 27/11/13)

BEGINNING & END

My Treaty of Rights
(In lamentation)

Just as I've taught you, everything has a right
Yet which were fulfilled with my own father's plight?
I've written a treaty… answered me tragedy
Hussain… Hussain

* * *

I've taught you that each, every thing has a right
And everything is precious in Islam's sight
And now, for my words, with my patience I fight
They laughed at my words, set my treaty alight

They laughed at my book and they burned its pages
And now, the head of my rights, a spear raises
I wrote them poetry… answered me tragedy
Hussain… Hussain

* * *

I begin speaking of the rights of a child
You must advise him and his character mould
And show him how he's a part of you in this world
If thirsty, don't let water from him be held

For O' listener I've seen children thirsty
The life from their eyes, thirst had taken away
I told them, let them be… answered me tragedy
Hussain… Hussain

* * *

I told Ali Akbar the rights of mothers
She'd feed you and clothed you when would no other
When thirsty you were for water worthier
Don't make Layla cry, go back and comfort her
I told this to him and Layla was watching
He turned away and left his mother crying

She'd cry out let him be… answered me tragedy
Hussain… Hussain

* * *

I told my uncle, your hand never extend
To what's forbidden from you, don't let it tend
Thirsty, when he held water within his hand
He threw it away, and with honour he'd stand
O' hands this water from you is forbidden
Don't touch it even if on dust you've fallen
The whole world, it would see… answered me tragedy
Hussain… Hussain

* * *

I tell you that have rights even your two eyes
What you shall see shall define your smiles and cries
How often to my eyes I'd apologize
In you, your father here upon the dust lies
The eyes they are the door to contemplation
The doors of my eyes saw my father fallen
For my eyes I'd worry… answered me tragedy
Hussain… Hussain

* * *

You father has rights, and for him be thankful
Comes from him, in you, anything beautiful
To my father his rights I'd explain and tell
And to his severed head I'd bid him farewell

The rights of my father I learnt and I knew
I burned him alone and told him thank you
I taught divine decree… answered me tragedy
Hussain… Hussain

* * *

(London – 15/12/12)

Where Are the Shia?

(In lamentation)

Monsoor, he calls out… "Where are the Shia?
Today we've murdered… their leader Jafar
Throw them in prison… find his successor"
They day they drew his shroud… Shia blood was allowed

* * *

What would be the darkest time in our history
Began with Jafar Al-Sadiq and his story
He built our school with golden teachings of glory
It challenged tyrants who for their rule would worry

Against oppressors… against all of them
His school, it glistened… a flag of freedom
Knowledge, it loved him… tyrants, they feared him
And after he stood proud… Shia blood was allowed

* * *

Al-Sadiq lived in a time where skies would darken
When our deaths became worship, not just oppression
A time where teachings of Mohammed were hidden
Where hiding our faith became half our religion

We live in danger… because we believe
Even we're safe… Shia elsewhere grieve
There is no freedom… if death we receive
Before to swords we bowed… Shia blood was allowed

* * *

Waging a war against the sons of Mohammed
The Abbasids waded in Shia blood they shed
Our blood flowed rivers till every house on it tread
To the door of the house of Jafar it was led

They sought his murder… killed every lover

An army waged war… against a scholar
Proving forever… knowledge is power
His knowledge cries aloud… Shia blood was allowed

* * *

Monsoor was amongst the greatest of oppressors
And took pride in killing the greatest of scholars
Everything innocent left in this world withers
Mourns him both orphaned children and widowed mothers

Today they bury… the last of their hope
Their grief can level… any mountain's slope
Knowledge, it laments… patience, it can't cope
As witnesses, a crowd… Shia blood was allowed

* * *

After his death we saw the last glimmer of day
As Monsoor cries "no more Shia after today"
Indeed since that day our freedom was locked away
Till our only hope was to for a return pray

Since then, killing us… was permissible
To have rights to life… we've not been able
We pray for Mehdi… "your promise fulfil"
Till the vengeance he vowed… Shia blood was allowed

* * *

(London – 26/02/14)

BEGINNING & END

King of Hearts
(In Celebration)

Once, from love ones torn apart… now king of millions of hearts
If any are left in sorrows, tell them: Ali Al-Ridha

* * *

Called a stranger, but not a stranger in our eyes
He comforts every heart where a stranger lies
They shy from all, but no stranger from his hand shies
And his hand wipes every tear that a stranger cries
A divine light that lights the heart's loneliest skies
In every stranger's heart, the flag of Ridha flies
Every stranger looks to him… the pride of Bani Hashim
Because to every stranger he is a friend and a father
If any are left in sorrows tell them: Ali Al-Ridha

* * *

Long after from Medina Al-Ridha was seized
He's yearned by the living and yearned by the deceased He who in his life, with anything, he was pleased
Leaves not a soul returning from his grave unpleased
Pleased with no family whilst by Ma'mun he's teased
With so many lovers now, can he be displeased?
Indeed "Ridha" he became… and named after his own name The eye weeps to think he smiled with no family member
If any are left in sorrows tell them: Ali Al-Ridha

* * *

Not allowed to upon his own home-soil tread
So Ridha lit up the whole of Meshhed instead
Taken away from the city of Mohammed
So in his grandfather's name he conquered Meshhed
From Medina to Meshhed, they wanted him dead
But from lovers to lovers Ridha they led
Take him in chains to Persia… take him handcuffed to China
Wherever he goes flock to him will lover after lover
If any are left in sorrows tell them: Ali Al-Ridha

* * *

Called a stranger as if no-one is lonelier

O' Ridha I swear I do not see a stranger
I see he who to some couldn't be dearer
To others dearer to them than their own mother
I see he who leaves no wish without an answer
I see a legend who entices forever
Like oceans to you they pour… extending hands by your door
Of the lonely and the beggar the lover and the carer
If any are left in sorrows tell them: Ali Al-Ridha

* * *

(London - 21/09/13)

BEGINNING & END

Jawad's Ship
(In Lamentation)

Another ship sets sail... upon its worship
Shrouded within black cloth... is Al-Jawad's ship
What a farewell... angels wail

* * *

Today it's not just the Shia... everything created is scarred
Anything that believes in God... is mourning for Imam Jawad
The oldest remember Kadhom... when mourned him the whole of Baghdad
Like Hussain on Karbala's plains... his lifeless body, lions guard

Again stories repeat... as which each Imam
Again an Imam killed... blood on tyrant's palm
Stories we tell... angels wail

* * *

Summoned to the land of Baghdad... as if to death he was summoned
Against the night of tyranny... like a star Al-Jawad glistened
Mutasim saw this and feared him... to this fear Um Fadhil listened
Till all of Baghdad heard a cry... "Imam Jawad has been poisoned"

Fed poison by his wife... like his grandfather
Angels cursed Um Fadhil... like Jamal's mother
Against evil... angels wail

* * *

An orphan at such a young age... just as his son upon him weeps
In his father's absence he grew... in his father's absence he sleeps
His hair grey from the pangs of grief... yet the title of "youth" he keeps
The ship of youth departs this world... as it sails, his tears it sweeps
The youngest ship sets sail... upon its own tears
Become both old and frail... have its youthful years
No more youthful... angels wail

* * *

Killed at the age of twenty-five… now millions for him have grieved
The under twenty-five should ask… "What exactly have I achieved"?
He conquered hearts and conquered youth… Ali Akbar in his blood weaved
The angel of death left surprised… when another youth he received
And how many angels… on his coffin weep
"Why does such a grand youth… in oppression sleep"?
His burial… angels wail

* * *

The ship of salvation departs… buried beside Musa Kadhom
The youth of the holy household… buried and youth buried with him
A gem sent a gift from the Lord… descended amongst men's mayhem
In yet another burial… his lovers rush to hide this gem
That familiar grief… that his lovers feel
Beside his burial… wails Jibraeel
With Jibraeel… angels wail

* * *

(London – 26/01/14)

Beginning & End

What Happened?
(In Lamentation)

How oppressed was your household… in Samarra what happened?
You led us for just six years… your son left for a thousand

* * *

There is a tale hidden in Samarra
It speaks of your oppression and your torture
It speaks of he who lived his life a prisoner
It speaks of an Imam led to his murder

Not just brought to Samarra… to your death you were summoned
You led us for just six years… your son left for a thousand

* * *

The son of orphans murdered as an orphan
Chosen by God yet to Samarra taken
What kind of age and what kind of oppression
When a divine king, a tyrant, would summon

Born in the darkest of times… a spark of light you glistened
You led us for just six years… your son left for a thousand

* * *

The caliph called you to show you his powers
By you paraded Samarra's best fighters
You asked him to look between your two fingers
Where he saw your hidden army of soldiers

By showing this miracle… he felt his power threatened
You led us for just six years… your son left for a thousand

* * *

It's not enough to prisons you were taken
They came to you and made your house a prison

Killing you easy, they wanted you broken
And ensured the sun of their time was hidden

They knew your words light up hearts… and made sure that few listened
You led us for just six years… your son left for a thousand

* * *

Even though away from the world you were torn
From the confines of your house scholars were born
By two things we've survived and this pride we've worn
By these scholars and by the Hussain we'd mourn

You set foundations for us… and the Shia you strengthened
You led us for just six years… your son left for a thousand

* * *

Indeed for your son, Mehdi, they'd been waiting
Just as his reappearance we're awaiting
They knew the twelfth prince, and knew his uprising
And wanted to kill him at his beginning

Yet they could not challenge God… nor challenge what was destined
You led us for just six years… your son left for a thousand

* * *

Fearing your knowledge, poisoned you Mu'tamid
Amongst fruits given to you poison he hid
Thirsty for blood of the sons of Mohammed
Jealous of the swords that tasted blood they've bled

Compared to the life you'd lived… your death for you was sweetened
You led us for just six years… your son left for a thousand

* * *

After you your son left for a thousand years
And in that time we can fill seas with our tears
O' Hassan we're killed and behind clouds he peers
We plead you by your name that he reappears

BEGINNING & END

O' Hassan it's been slaughter… since the day you were poisoned
You led us for just six years… your son left for a thousand

* * *

(London – 26/02/14)

THE AWAITED

Poetry in memory of the Twelfth Imam

(May the Almighty hasten his reappearance)

"And when we stand by our beloved, we'll remember
We'd read Ahad each day and each Friday Nudba"

Before I Leave
(In lamentation)

Before I leave this world… I want to see the Mehdi

* * *

O' Lord I raise my hands and I cry out a prayer
For years I've watched the age in my eyes, away, wear
These two eyes have never seen hope, only despair
And they're complaining that his absence is unfair

Can I argue with them… they've seen only tragedy

* * *

I paint to you a picture and paint it in tears
To the absence of my beloved, I've sold my years
And I've lived every day hoping he reappears
Since a young age I've known only trials and fears

Every trial and test… calls for the son of Ali

* * *

O' Lord I swear by the carer of his neighbour
His enemies our conviction will outnumber
And when we stand by our beloved, we'll remember
We'd read Ahad each day and each Friday Nudba

The pain in which he lived… will be but a memory

* * *

I ask for the return of the 'rightly guided'
As tells me Ahad when in it I've confided
If after forty days my place is decided
Must I wait forty years to, by him, be aided?

After forty mornings… must I still cry "I'm ready"?

* * *

It scares me my eyes were born without him in sight
It scares me more they may not see him till my plight
Lord you request for our faith to be at its height
Since birth, my eyes are yet to adjust to his sight

I swear I'll never sin… if I see his face daily

* * *

O' Lord every Friday has become a torture
We call out his name and do not hear an answer
Every Friday, Heavens and Earth shout together
"Where's the avenger of the killed in Karbala?"

And Friday's sunset weeps… knowing next week it will pray

* * *

I ask You to promise me O' Merciful Lord
When I die and indeed death for all is assured
With his return raise me from my grave with my sword
With the sight of my beloved my only reward

Don't let even my death… come between his rise and me

* * *

London – 09/09/13

Which Door?

(In lamentation)

Every door that's closed, they say another one opens
Which one do we close for Mehdi to reawaken?
Which door... will return you?
We're still... waiting for you... to reawaken

* * *

O' love that sleeps in my heart as a beloved
O' he who wants nothing more than to be loved
Know that not a day passes when you're unloved
Centuries have passed, but you are still beloved

If centuries pass, the most loved on is forgotten
Yet a thousand years and you remain unforgotten
Daily... we recall you
We're still... waiting for you... to reawaken

* * *

Our patience has not been defeated by time
But we've known nothing but pain in our lifetime
Our love for you itself has become a crime
Will you leave us waiting till the end of time?

I can't exaggerate when I tell you O' Master
We've become the herd that wolves look for just to slaughter
Aidless... we await you
We're still... waiting for you... to reawaken

* * *

Could it be that nothing awakes you from sleep?
When even the heedless can't sleep when we weep
And our tears, thousands of angels come to sweep
We tell them, till he comes, our tears let us keep

We hold onto tears, and from our hands, they are dripping

Every tear that falls, asks is the Mehdi still sleeping?
Each tear… cries out to you
We're still… waiting for you… to reawaken

* * *

How often a hatred on us is imposed
And door after door upon us has been closed
Yet your open door to us was not proposed
And alone, for you, injustice we opposed

Inflicted with grief, Mehdi, I asked you a question
Even if we found your door, your door would you open?
Must we… come and find you
We're still… waiting for you… to reawaken

* * *

So in love, that we had arguments with fate
Would you make a lover for his beloved wait?
And his absence crushes our hearts with its weight
The day these hearts are destroyed, do you await?

How we're told that fate, closes doors and so opens doors
Yet your door is closed, though on it a sea of tears pours
Does fate… understand you?
We're still… waiting for you… to reawaken

* * *

Enough waiting, just show us toward your door
If you need lovers, millions to you pour
If you need a key, we'll break open this door
O' loner, know your name, millions adore

A letter of hope I seal and, in the wind, send
Don't keep us waiting, for we shall wait until time's end
Reply… I request you
We're still… waiting for you… to reawaken

* * *

London – 19/02/13

In Mehdi's Eyes
(In lamentation)

We see in your eyes… tears of blood you cry

* * *

O' twelfth Imam we gaze into the eyes that we've adored
And see, illustrated, pictures from which your tears have poured
Daily you recall broken ribs, poison, arrows and sword
Your eyes bear such a weight that blood from your veins it has lured

Daily you're taunted… by tales haunted

* * *

Your grief has left a road to history, which we follow
We see, upon a woman's grief, left a house of sorrow
She mourns her father, a river of tears draws her shadow
A withered rose when once in her father's hand she would grow

She cries and laments… sorrowful moments

* * *

I wonder what picture would make blood from your two eyes pour
Could it be seeing, daily, the attack on your mother?
The witnesses to this O' Mehdi, in your eyes are four:
The mother and the crushed infant between the wall and door

A distress, endless… daily you witness

* * *

Beyond what you see, daily O' Mehdi you hear thunder
The sound of the strike of the sword on the head of Haider
The deafening call "Islam's pillars are destroyed" you hear
You tell this voice, your heart demolishes which each pillar

With each pillar crushed… your wailing is hushed

* * *

I watch the blood that trickles from the torment of your eyes
And see, that for a forgotten uncle, your eye, it cries
Alone, abandoned, forgotten and poisoned, Hassan dies
You remember him when your eyes, not a single hand dries

Weeps for you, Hassan… like you, an orphan

* * *

Whilst the tears of your eyes dry up and take from your bloodstream
Into your hands O' last orphan the tears of mothers stream
Layla wails over Ali Akbar in a harsh dream
Rabab burns out a candle crying out "O' my Jassim"

And Ramla wails… swaying a cradle

* * *

You're thirsty for your lovers as the days like decades pass
The blood you have to cry, all the tragic tales surpass
You come to drink water and your hand shakes holding its glass
"May God have His mercy upon my uncle Al Abbas"

You hear him daily… "forgive me Ali"

* * *

I ask you O' grieving loner of the root of your pain
Alone he lies, fallen, whilst none of his household remain
Your eyes behind the clouds cause tears of blood to, on him, rain
They cry, "This headless, trampled body belongs to Hussain"

Upon your beloved… you cry tears of blood

* * *

Grief grips your body like poison, as if stories you've heard
As if it's heard tales of Baqir, Sadiq and Sajjad
Could it be that fate says you'll come but go against its word?

BEGINNING & END

Just like it released Kathom as a body in Baghdad

Poisoned hearts wander… if you'll come ever

* * *

Mehdi you find yourself a stranger wherever you stand
You weep for Ridha killed as a stranger in a strange land
Could it be that age tortures you like tide eats away sand?
You recall Jawad poisoned in his youth by tyrant's hand

* * *

Millions ask where you reside, into nights you've faded
Where did you stand when the two Askaris' dome exploded?
Mehdi what else could have your thousand-year absence ended?
Daily Baqi' cries out your name begging to be mended

Even broken graves… your return they crave

* * *

I watch the sun rise, daily, asking if, you, it will bring
And find the fate of your return weaved deep in my being
I thank my Lord that the Ahlulbayt are my everything
I tell Him for my last beloved, my eyes are still waiting

Bearing such a weight… your rise we await

* * *

(London – 05/07/13)

Ali's Door

The night's shroud falls, though it seems too early
The sun departs, but is it not too early?
I raise my sorrows within my hands to Ali
I have come begging at your door O' Haider

You know your name is fused in my bloodstream
Unhesitant, it flows in my bloodstream
You see my tears flow harshly, as if my blood streams
And would you dare turn away such a lover?

I'll knock on your door gently and not harder
Your help as easy as a prayer, not harder
Who would turn a beggar away? Not Haider
Can I knock your door without reply? Never

He whose name flows in me, a flame
You'd rush to soothe me, if burnt me a flame
I've come to your door with my whole heart aflame
You'd help a neighbour, am I just a neighbour?

I seek the shade from darkness in the light
And the comfort of Ali's touch, in the light
And the smile of my beloved in delight
Seeing my happy that my pleas he'd answer

Knocking your door is but the beginning
It's in grief that all smiles begin in
Please O' Haider Karrar, I'm begging
Would you leave me here asking forever?

* * *

Imam Mehdi

I see in the day, the moon's rays don't belong
Just as the tears in your eyes don't belong
I plead to you O' beloved, don't be long
So much is out of place without you, Master

Yearns for a stronger heart, a weakened one
When will this heart no more be a weakened one?
O' Lord let return the awakened one
Let him strengthen hearts that without him are weaker

On the place of your abode, I wonder
Drawn on the lens of my eye, wonder
In the day's lack of light, I wander
When will your beauty I witness O' Master?

The Earth's lack of light, daily, I witness
I feel upon my cheek, a wetness
And with everything that my eyes witness
They don't see the rise of the son of Karrar

I await the flickers of your sunlight
O' Mehdi, your moon heavy and your sun light
Indeed you are your mother's son - light
The Lady of Light prays for you to appear

Your absence has left minds in confusion
We cannot percieve you with such confusion
Belief percieves you but, Mehdi, can vision?
The eye aches to see belief in a true picture

O' Mehdi know very well what "judge" meant
Its definition no longer what "judge" meant
I plead O' Mehdi, return, pass your judgement
On those who see justice as our slaughter

I can't tell you why this yearning is, it just is
I can't say how patience is dying, it just is
Return and soothe our patience, it's justice
To us and to those who ask if you'll come ever

There is cause and effect with every action
Whilst you watch, daily, our every action
We plead daily but don't see a reaction
Heed us and rise up O' son of Fatima

In your absence to our prayers you react
We plead for help, from the shadows you react
O' Mehdi return, then your miracles re-act
Only infront of our eyes, O' beloved saviour

In the absence of my beloved so impatient
Centuries of waiting made me so impatient
But I know you haven't forgotten, so I'm patient
O' Mehdi don't let my patience become torture

In the ink of my wishes, today, I dress
I write a letter and, you, I address
To which house do I send it? Which address?
I send it in the wind and await your answer

* * *

Ashura

(Muharram)
A month that causes millions to suffer
Yet they yearn for its rise, to suffer
And continue their mourning from Muharram to Safar
Mourning the story of each martyr's Master

The day rises yet watches the night fall
Onto tormented hearts would this night fall
As Muharram begins with the nightfall
As the hearts that love him welcome their torture

(Fatima Al-Aleela)
Father go to Mecca and no further
Don't get to Nainawa and say "no... Further!"
I'm scared Karbala will leave me with and no father
And I'm scared it will leave me an orphaned daughter

(Ruqaya)
Beneath the tears of her eyes, a sweet heart

BEGINNING & END

The pangs of sorrow grip her sweet heart
"Lord hasten the return of my sweetheart.
if he asks 'who's asking?' Tell him Ruqaya"

(Ummul Baneen)
How many mothers have, four, given
And left the killers of her sons, forgiven
But the killers of Hussain? Unforgiven
Daily she'll pray for the rise of his avenger

A story that's a school for lessons
In her house she has raised four lessons
Her sacrifice left her with four less sons
No Abbas, Abdullah, Uthman nor Jafar

It is You who taught us what a judge meant
O' peak of justice, pass your judgement
I hold two severed hands for your judgement
I complain to you Lord, of Bani Umaya

Tender in mercy, punishment you're harsh in
Show me Mercy, their judgement be harsh in
I ask you Lord as a servant of Bani Hashim
For what sin was my son killed in Karbala?

I can't forgive them and I've cried forever
Hussain's my son and will be forever
Avenge him O' Lord, but not my four, ever
They were gifts to my son, the son of Fatima

(Muslim Ibn Aqeel)
What a bitter feeling, no sweetness, no honey
No food to eat, no milk and no honey
No friend & you want me alive? No, Haani
Tell Ibn Ziyad to kill me here in Kufa

(Ansar)
Against human intellect and willpower
A revolution our blood will power
And the legacy of Hussain we'll power
From Aabis to John to Habib Al-Muthahir

(Abbas)

NOURI SARDAR

Sit next to me my son, I'm your father
Zainab is worth so much to your father
Don't protect her till death, go further
Even after death make sure your flag guards her

Your eyes and your glare no soul saw past
Walking with Zainab, whoever you saw, passed
Their heads bowed, your zeal none surpassed
What zeal! Even in death your flag guards her

Against the rift of thousands, two gather
From the sons of Mohammed and Ali, two gather
O' Abbas if we fall, we fall together
Hold my back and I'll hold yours O' flagbearer

They watch from his hand, the water fall
Between selflessness and the river a waterfall
And the fall that he had what a fall
Only selflessness falls before his banner

(Ramla)
Ramla close your eyes, you have a visitor
Open your tent and embrace this visitor
On the day of days, would would visit her?
It's your martyred beloved, so wail O' Ramla

(Layla)
A mother and a painful memory I recall
Raising my hands to my Lord my eyes recall
I send him away but then my son I recall
You returned Yusuf, return him to his mother

(Imam Hussain)
A picture in your sorrow you would draw
With your infant's blood, revolution you would draw
You cry O' Ali and your sword you withdraw
And the thousands descend on the son of Karrar

Who can find his immortality as suprising
With him I find that nothing is suprising
Even after death, you see that his uprising
Has toppled dictator after dictator

BEGINNING & END

Ziyarat Karbala

(Ziyarat Al-Hussain)

The language of love, your love rewords
"My love" into "longing for you" rewords
When I serve you, I know its rewards
A visit to your grave in Karbala

When your comfort and presence I adore
My visits to you, always, I adore
I picture a courtyard and a door
The door to the grave of my Master

I recall my spirit's rise and ascent
The lover's heart's comfort and ascent
I recall a feeling and a scent
That I feel next to you Aba Abdillah

I recall a beautiful shrine, its content
I feel at home with its wonderful content
I feel comforted, understood and content
Beneath a grand dome upon which flies, your banner

And there, whatever I wish or announce
With impossible dreams I'd seek or announce
I'd not feel a shred of doubt, or an ounce
That whatever I'd request he'd grant and answer

Within my heart days have turned to night
Two lights once in my heart became two nights
How I wish that I was by them tonight
By Hussain and by his brother, the flagbearer

Perhaps all that we see is real
But you can't see yearning, yet it's so real
My dreams mean nothing next to a dream surreal
I wish I was beside Hussain in Karbala

He, when from grief our hair we wouldn't dye, mends
He, all that in the heart would die, mends
He's worth more than gold and diamonds

And his dust became medicine in his honour

Never came close to knowing his worth, gold
And weeps at the scale of his worth, gold
If anyone told you that he's worth gold
Tell them even Heaven's gold knows its Master

(Ziyarat Al-Abbas)

You sit, a hidden diamond before me
I know you know my wishes before me
And all the dreams that would be for me
You let loose from your hand, to me they flutter

You wish and however difficult your wish is
Just tell Abu Fadhil what your wish is
Don't think they're impossible, your wishes
You'll upset the best door to your desire

None will percieve his virtues or his content
Millions are entranced by his content
And he who understands Abbas, he is content
For he has the greatest helper as his helper

(Karbala)

I'm still wondering what I met her for
With the years since I first met her, four
I likened her to a beloved, my metaphor
As in her absence I cry her name, "Karbala"

Remnants within my hand of what I crush
The most beautiful rose is what I crush
I crush it because I'm in love, what a crush
In love with what I hold: the dust of Karbala

* * *

Path of the Ahlulbayt

The Quran to Mohammed, what a revelation
A verse to appoint Ali, what a revelation
Revolutionized by Hussain, and what a revolution

BEGINNING & END

A revolution held on each Shia banner

O' sunrise the night's shroud tells you, you're early
O' sunrise of hope I know why you're early
I began my day saying "Ya Ali"
And found the father of dust my greatest helper

There's never a morning too early
Because I wake to the greatest ally
Daily I wake and salute Ali
And tell him at your service today/forever

Daily I wake, I tell you O' Ali with you
You stole our loyalty, took it O' Ali with you
I face a problem, my mother says "Ali's with you"
I say Ali's with me and Hussain's flagbearer

In blaming our love they seek to perfect
Our hearts & our minds they want to perfect
His love has no imperfection. Ali's too perfect
Imperfect is the one who hates the Shia

A weighty thing on the eye weighted
All my life, to see their beauty I waited
Beginning with Ahmed, ending with the awaited
Two weighty things, one of them is heavier

I, with a belief drawn on my eye, succeeded
Only one can say "Mohammed I succeeded"
And he cried out when he was struck, "I succeeded!"
I too succeed in following Haider Karrar

* * *

A Beloved
A beloved and never can I lie to her
To the flame of my emotions, a lighter
She demolishes ego, makes my heart lighter
She's the ink of my pen that makes verses of wonder
Into the depths of my heart, daily, I peek
Of mountains that are verses of love, a peak
The love between beloved & lover, its peak
The urge to write for the house of Fatima

In my heart I built a nation, what a state
It yearns verses I may speak and what I state
The state their love left me in, what a state
Make my pen ageless, I'll write in the hereafter
It swayed my heart and changed me mentally
I think verses and lines, almost mentally
Whenever I wrote "love", I meant "Ali"
And when I say "Ali" I mean أولاد و علي
Whenever I thought "purpose", "Ali" it succeeded
I saw that Mohammed, only he succeeded
My pen loved his name, that's why it succeeded
Take his name off the page, it's just ink on paper

Pages, each with the love of Ali weighted
Volumes, the weight of each toward Ali fated
'Fate' is as words for him and his sons, elevated
Thank you Lord for the greatest job and honour

ABOUT THE WRITER

In Brief

"Let me speak to you of the pen that I use to write…
…and of the ink that I use to build houses of might…"

Nouri Sardar is an established and published poet. He has published 4 books as volumes collecting his written poetry. A spoken word artist, he has performed in various cities in the UK, Europe, Middle East, Canada and the United States (the latter including states such as California, Michigan, Florida, New York, New Jersey and Maryland). He has worked on multiple spoken word tracks including 2 albums in collaboration with the reciter Ali Fadhil. He has also written for numerous reciter and lecturers. After studying film and television studies, he works at Ahlulbayt TV as a television producer and director.

Style

"Building a poem is no different to houses men build,
It's a structure, yet instead of brick, syllables you wield,
Because the mind loves perfection, and I find my mind filled,
With a thousand ideas, but it's all about how you weld,
Words how you want them to be…"

Poetry being a vast subject, his writings can best be described as the art of poetry mixed with the art of hymns. His writing holds an evident poetic heart and foundation, but follows structures defined by syllables and rhyme. Inspired by poetry written in the East in various languages, his poetry is romantic, and seeks to meddle with the hearts and emotions of the readers and listeners.

Theme

"In how many ways can you narrate a well-known story,
Yet without taking away its honour and its glory?
A picture says a thousand words, but look to poetry,
It paints pictures in the mind where housed is thought and theory,
Where emotions are conflicted by grief and by worry,
Where told is man to smile, cry or be engulfed by fury…"

The vast majority of Nouri's writings are in honour and reverence of the holy household of the Prophet Muhammad (peace and blessings be upon him and his family).

His poetry is divided into poems written in lamentation of their sufferings and tragedies, and poems written in celebration of their existence, births and characters. However, it is not a clear-cut divide, with the overall aim of his writing to both instil and inflame the love for these historic personalities in hearts, with the goal that readers and listeners may benefit from the eternal lessons that string from the perfect and just morality embedded in this household, all via poetics.

Audience

"…With a poem, everything must be in its proper place,
Yet distorted, yet beautiful, so that eyes can retrace,
Each carefully welded word to my heart, its birthplace,
Feelings and ideas that tend to transcend both time and space…"

Nouri's volumes of poetry seek to provide for the wide gap of English poetry written in praise of the Ahlulbayt (peace and blessings be upon them all). They can be heard and read by any lover of peace, justice and goodness, by the lovers of poetry, creative writing, the religious and non-religious, the Muslim and the non-Muslim. Furthermore, the poems also provide reciters and lecturers with poems to recite in honour of the holy Household.

"With writing a poem, you feel your words are jailed
In your mind and you try to make sense of them before unveiled
Are the feelings of your heart, laid out for the world detailed
And man by his words has either fallen or has prevailed…"

"So what you shall read in these pages are the feelings of my own heart, emotion, and mode of thinking. It is not written for the critical eye, it has no underlining political agenda, it is not written to cause friction and disunity, it is written purely and sincerely for the service of this great Household; it is written as a letter from me to my masters that are this holy Household; it is written to paint a picture in your mind as I have imagined it, and thus the words you shall find scattered throughout this book are written from my heart to yours." – Nouri Sardar, excerpt from Vol. 2

The Poet Online:

Official website: www.NouriSardar.com
Twitter: @NouriSardar
Facebook: http://www.facebook.com/nourisardar
Contact: Nouri.Sardar@Gmail.com

ABOUT THE PUBLISHER

UMAA was founded in 2002, and is currently one of the largest Shia Ithna Asheri organizations in North America. Over the past twelve years, UMAA has grown significantly as an organization and hopes to better serve the needs of our community. This year's Grand Iftar, with all of our wonderful guests this evening, is a reflection of our desire to, not only grow, but to our desire to advance in the way that our Holy Prophet (PBUH) wanted us to.

UMAA hosts one of the largest annual gatherings of Shias in North America, attended by thousands of individuals from across the country and around the world. In 2015, the UMAA Convention will be held in the great city of Chicago, and I invite each of you to attend.

UMAA has been quite active on a variety of humanitarian issues. UMAA has hosted clothing and blanket drives, raising tens of thousands of dollars for the poor and misfortunate of Iraq. Currently, we are sponsoring the Ummul Baneen School in Najaf, Iraq – the city's only English language children's school. UMAA has also opened a high school in Azad Kashmir to help develop the growing community.

The organization has opened one of the largest Shia Muslim digital libraries in the world: the Sheikh Tusi Digital Library, so that you can benefit from the brightest writers in Islamic history. Our team regularly contributes to columns in the Washington Times and other major internet news providers. UMAA is also producing high quality digital, audio and video content.

Printed in Great Britain
by Amazon